The Caboodles blueprint

Turn Your Idea Into Millions

LEONIE MATEER

The Caboodles Blueprint
Copyright © 2013 by Leonie Mateer. All rights reserved.

No part of this publication may be reproduced, stored in a retrieval system or transmitted in any way by any means, electronic, mechanical, photocopy, recording or otherwise without the prior permission of the author except as provided by USA copyright law.

This book is designed to provide accurate and authoritative information with regard to the subject matter covered. This information is given with the understanding that the author is not engaged in rendering legal, professional advice. Since the details of your situation are fact dependent, you should additionally seek the services of a competent professional.

Published in the United States of America

ISBN : 978-09987014-0-0

1. Business & Economics/Development/General
2. Business & Economics/Marketing/General

1st Edition: 12.11.12
2nd Edition: 01.02.17

Leonie Mateer is a marketing wizard. In my fifteen years in the magazine business, I never met anyone who could create and market a product as well as Ms. Mateer. When I was at TEEN Magazine we became partners in creating, marketing, special advertising sections, and events to make Caboodles a household name. Read this book and learn the secrets from the master of marketing.

> Nancy Ryburn, Former Director
> of Special Projects, TEEN Magazine.

Endorsements

I had the pleasure of working with Leonie Mateer on her first major product launch in the United States; Caboodles cosmetic organizers. She brought a vast knowledge of product development and a unique and fresh approach to marking her product. I watched Ms. Mateer turn a new concept of a cosmetic organizer into a household name and one owned by the vast majority of teenagers in the United States. I was very proud to be a part of the marketing team that spear headed the launch of Caboodles at Target nationally. I can unequivocally state that it was one of the most exciting times in my whole business career. Caboodles was one of the most successful and smashing successes in history – thanks to a Sr. Buyer who recognized the enormous potential this brand brought to their stores. If you are looking to take a new product concept to market, I whole-heartedly recommend you read this book before you take your fist step.

      Connie Trueman, Steubs-Trueman, Inc.
      a sales and marketing agency

Dedication

To my daughters, Toni and Amie
who have always been my inspiration

Table of Contents

Introduction --- 8
Visualization --- 13
Won't My Product Idea Be Stolen? --------------------- 26
Developing Your Product Profile ----------------------- 31
Developing Your Packaging ------------------------------ 43
Defining Your Consumer Target Market --------------52
Learn From Your Focus Groups ------------------------54
Research Makes You the Expert ------------------------66
Setting Up Your Rep Force ------------------------------ 86
Licensing Your Product ---------------------------------106
Creating Your Brand -------------------------------------109
Expanding Your Vision --------------------------------- 122
Creating Your Product Line ----------------------------125
Taking Your Product from Paper to Prototype---- 130
Packaging Design --142
POP In Store Display Vehicles ------------------------146
Choosing Your Manufacturer------------------------- 153
Pricing Your Product ----------------------------------- 166
Sales Materials and Sales Calls ----------------------- 177
Marketing Your Product -------------------------------- 182
Time to Do Your Check List ---------------------------194
Going On Your "Road Show" ------------------------- 197

Do You Have A Viable Product?	208
Trade Shows	213
Establishing Yourself in the Marketplace	222
The Changing Face of Retail	226
Licensing Your Brand Name	231
How Much Does It Cost?	235
Conclusion	249
About the Author	251

Introduction

If you are reading this book there is a good chance that you have a product or an idea you want to "take to market" and make a fortune doing it.

I can't promise that you will make a fortune, but I can assist you with taking your product concept and making it a reality. Whether or not you make a fortune will depend on the end consumer. I have taken what I thought were brilliant product ideas to market only to discover the consumer didn't share the same enthusiasm for the product as I did. Hence, a financial disaster was waiting for me at the end of my journey. I have since learned to "listen" to my focus groups and, if we do not get over 85 percent acceptance, then it is time to come up with a new product idea.

Most of my products, however, have become very successful. New and improved product ideas that I brought to market twenty-five years ago can still be seen sitting on the shelves of thousands of retails stores and available at major online retailers throughout the world.

There is nothing more rewarding than seeing your product in the marketplace and knowing it is selling. Nothing is more exciting than seeing a consumer using your product. I was sitting in an airport in Mexico one afternoon and there, seated a few seats down from me, was a girl with a Caboodles™ cosmetics case sitting on her lap. She had it open and was using the mirror to check her makeup. She had it filled with all her precious things. It was like watching my dream come true. She looked so happy.

This book is not about my successes or my failures, but what I have learned along the way. You don't need a marketing degree to understand how to take your product to market but you do need to know what steps to take along the way.

I am a New Zealander who has lived the American dream; a self-educated product developer and marketer. I have been an entrepreneur since I was fifteen-years-old – the age when I left home and high school full of enthusiasm to enter the working world. Three years of a New Zealand high school had provided me with excellent skills in bookkeeping, typing and shorthand. So, armed with my mother's positive attitude and my older sister's hand-me-down clothes, I began my journey.

I was, most likely, born an entrepreneur. My daughter, Amie, who got her MBA in her early twenties and has continued on to be a successful Senior Director of Marketing for a major US company, said to me once "Mum, you may not know the correct marketing names for what you do, you just do it."

This is a book about "just doing it" - taking your idea and turning it into a reality.

My expertise is in creating products and brands, and marketing and selling to the mass market industry. No matter where your product's final resting place will be – this book is a good start to getting it on its way.

When I first saw a fishing tackle box used as a cosmetics organizer I didn't have the vision. I was busy in my New Zealand model agency and hardly noticed a model who arrived late for a shoot one day. She was armed with an old metal fishing tackle box all neatly organized with her collection of beauty aids.

It was only after I had been living in the USA for six months, and was looking for a fishing tackle box to organizer my own cosmetics, that I had the vision. Right here, crouched on the floor of a Thrifty drug store excitedly opening up all the different styles of plastic fishing tackle boxes with their amazing swing back trays and compartments, at that moment my vision was born.

It was November 1986, when I decided to turn my vision into a reality. It was June 1987, when we first launched Caboodles™ cosmetics organizer boxes into the marketplace. Over twenty years later, these brightly colored boxes are still adorning the shelves of major retailers worldwide and available online in multiple shapes and sizes at the world's number one online retailer.

When I decided to create a product and get it distributed I searched through libraries and bookshops for this book. It didn't exist. Marketing books were too complicated. I wanted to read a book from someone who had actually taken a product to market. I wanted to know where to start and what to do. I wanted a simple blueprint. I cannot tell you if your product is going to be the next big Hoola-Hoop™, Cabbage Patch Doll™, or iPhone™ but I can tell you how to take your vision and, if it is accepted by the industry, how to get it on the retail shelves.

Caboodles™ is the first of many product lines I have successfully taken to market. The successful introduction of each and every product is the direct result of applying the principle of the caboodles blueprint.

No matter what your idea is – an innovative picture frame or a unique cleaning service – this book will be a great starting place to work on your brand image, how to focus your idea with your potential consumers, and assist you with achieving your end result – your product in the marketplace.

I would suggest reading the whole book first and then going back to the chapters that relate specifically to your product or idea when you are ready to take your journey to success.

The only qualifications you need to bring your product to market are; tenacity, hard work and knowledge. Combine these with a positive attitude, a sense of humor, and a vision and you are ready to begin.

Visualization

Visualization is the Most Important Ingredient for a Product's Success

As you walk down the isle of a mass retail store and look at the thousands of products on the shelves you can rest assured that every one of those products started with a vision.

Go Shopping

The first step in expanding your vision is taking your product idea and visually placing it on the shelves in a retail store. Visit a store that would sell your product. Walk the isles, choose a space to put your product. Look at prices of similar type products. Are the products pegs and hanging on hooks or are they sitting on the shelves? What type of packaging are they using? What colors are other products? How many different styles are there? What color is the packaging? What color is the product? What space in the store is dedicated to your type of item?

Are there similar items sold in different places throughout the store? What is the category called that "houses" your type of items (e.g. toys, sporting goods, cosmetic)? Ask a store person what items are selling the best and what prices sell the best. I often explain that I am shopping for a teenage niece and want to buy her the "coolest product." Take lots of notes or use a voice recorder.

You may be wondering why visualization is so important in the early stages of your product's development. Visualization is the first step to taking your idea from a mere thought in your mind to its place in the real world. Finding the right "home" for your product is imperative in its future development. By having the visual of your product sitting on the store shelf, and knowing where it belongs, you will be surprised how easy it is to get it there.

Expand Your Idea

The second step in your visualization process is multiplication. One product usually has a life span of eighteen months on a store shelf. Very seldom do you make money on a single item in its first introduction. By the time it has hit the shelves, retail buyers are looking for what's new. Sometimes it is as simple as reintroducing the item in a new color. Often the original product idea is not the "best seller". The best selling item is often a hybrid of the original concept.

In order to capture shelf space in a retail store it is much more attractive to a buyer, and much more credible to the industry if you take your product concept and expand it into a product line. For example; three different price points, three different colors, and, if the product allows, a number of different styles. The optimum result is to have a "line of products" that will fill a two foot or four foot area in the store. You will be working on this portion of your product development in the "expanding your product into a product line" section of this book.

Do Your Homework

The third step in visualization is documenting your knowledge. As you go through the different stages of development you will be collating, organizing and filing this information away for later use. Your mind will also be automatically incorporating this information into your vision. A vision is never stagnant; it is a living, breathing entity. A stagnant vision is a dead vision.

If you can visualize it – you can make it. I have always been a believer that thought concretizes. The power of thought and using this power has been the root of my success. Many years ago a physicist whom I met while creating a new product line, asked me to be part of a new group of physicists who were studying the effects of thought solidifying. I was much too intimidated to participate in their theory with my meager high school education, but they said that I lived this theory every day. I can tell you that I do know that a vision, or thought, that is nurtured and developed in the mind, will simply dissipate if your focus is removed from it.

Do not underestimate the power of your mind. Your vision will materialize; all you need are the tools to develop it.

During your initial research stage take advantage of the web. Have you researched online for images and products that resemble your idea? Does it exist already? Now is the time to find out.

Caboodles™ introduction preceded the online

shopping phenomenon, so "getting on the shelf" in a retailers' store was our main focus. Today the major mass retailers are marketing their own online retail sites. Over the past couple of decades, online shopping has been growing in leaps and bounds. Some interesting statistics from the Wall Street Journey indicate that about 190 million US consumers – more than half the population – will shop online in 2016 with Amazon being one of the biggest game changers. There is no doubt that having, an presence online allows you to take advantage of the web's virtually infinite product range.

Creatively Recording and Documenting the Vision

When I began my product development journey it was before Photoshop and Illustrator, and I spent a fortune on graphic artists trying to document my visions. Not only have these computer programs saved me tens of thousands of dollars in the development process, but have given me the freedom and the control to capture my vision on paper and keep it updated as new information is gathered.

Everyone wants to know, "how much it will cost to take a product to market?" As we continue throughout the different stages I will explain what development are involved and what choices you can make depending on your financial situation. I will always give you the most cost effective way, which is usually utilizing your existing skills or newly developed skills.

Product development has never been as cost effective as it is now. Computer design programs, online research, free downloads of legal documents and contracts and online companies such as fiverr.com who offer graphic design and writing services at extremely low cost, have enabled do it yourself product inventors to save literally hundreds of thousands of dollars in development costs.

Take Control of Your Vision

I am a true entrepreneur, which means I participate in every stage of the development process myself. You do not need to have trained as a graphic artist, because with the computer programs available today, you can execute everything you need to turn your vision into a viable product. At the very least you can put your vision on paper and take it through the first stage of development very inexpensively and effectively. Look into night classes or online classes at local colleges to learn the basics if the task of teaching yourself is too daunting.

We still use creative designers to create our final logos and execute our trade and consumer ads and, when required, we also used product designers to put the final touches on product designs. I had the pleasure of working with a wonderful product designer during the product development of both Caboodles™ and Sassaby™ organizer boxes.

The more you can do yourself, the less expensive it is in the early stages. You may, however, need some assistance along the way until you become proficient with your computer programs.

Keep costs to a minimum as a lot of the initial work is purely conceptual and is only in the research stage of development and not seen by anyone else but you.

Although "go shopping" means checking out your competition to find out where their products are placed in the store, what items are selling the best etc., you don't want to let their product features influence your initial creative process. It is imperative that your creative process is not tainted by outside influences in the early stages. This could result in your product losing its innovative qualities and its value.

If your product is a "service product" check out similar services. Don't just Google search; check out what similar services are provided in your neighborhood. Ask your friends and neighbors what products or services they use.

No One Has All the Answers

The biggest waste of time in your product's early development is expecting that there is someone out there who knows more than you do. Someone, that you can simply call up and ask all those questions to (even if you do know what questions to ask) and expect them to give you all the answers. Wrong. No one is out there, believe me.

You will become the expert in your field. There is no fairy godmother disguised as a "new product promoter and developer" – often just costly imposters. No one will be able to sell your product to the marketplace better than you. And no one will give it the attention it needs more than you.

Your vision is your gift and it belongs to you. It was given to you to do with as you choose.

Choosing the Tools To Capture the Vision

If you don't have a personal computer and a color printer, buy them. You will need them for product concept, product development and research.

The software you will need is Photoshop, Acrobat Reader, PowerPoint and, of course, word.

Photoshop will enable you to take your photos, scanned images and rough drawings and manipulate them to best resemble your product idea. Photoshop is an ideal program for creating all your initial product concepts. I also use Photoshop for many of my sales materials and online graphics for my social media sites.

Acrobat Reader allows you to download documents for research and download necessary legal documents such as; confidentiality agreements, independent contractor agreements, talent release forms and sales representative agreements and, further down the line when your product is a great success, licensing agreements.

PowerPoint enables you to create sales presentations and business presentations and Word is your program for day-to-day record keeping, press releases, etc. Word also has layouts for booklet catalogs, photo catalogs, brochures, business cards, posters, signs and so much more.

If you think you would like to be more involved in producing your sales catalogs and promotional materials, then Illustrator™ is a program I have used. Access to the web is also crucial for your product research and graphic assistance.

Find someone who can use these programs and have the sit with you to show you the basic tools. You will learn with practice. Take a class if you feel you should. I am still saying, twenty-five years later, I should take a class, however I tend to develop my skills through practice and trial and error.

If you can only afford one program, start with Photoshop. This is the program you will be working with the most throughout the product development process.

You will need a good digital camera. The quality of digital cameras today has eliminated huge photography costs previously associated with the product development process. This tool enables you to update your photography as your product develops. It is a one-time cost that pays for itself over and over again. It also gives you control over the end result.

A good friend of mine, and a successful entrepreneur, once gave me the best advice regarding investing in the equipment you need for your business. He said. "Don't ever hesitate to invest in the tools you need to do your job. Without the right tools, you can never perfect the job." To this day, I don't hesitate to update my software and equipment. The better your tools, the better the end result.

To Do List

Visit at least four retail stores (both online and in-store) that carry your type of item. Then answer these questions:

What category would your item be placed in?

What packaging was used on similar products?

How many different styles/shapes of products (that resemble your product) were there?

How many different prices were there for your type of items?

What price do you think your product should be (based on similar products in the store)

How much shelf space was dedicated to your type of item?

What was the best selling item in your product category? (Store personnel input.)

Homework:

Based on your store research:

How many colors could you make your product idea in?

How many sizes could you make your product idea in?

How many different variations of your product idea could you make?

Check List:

• Hardware: computer, color printer, digital camera, voice recorder

- Software programs: Photoshop, Acrobat Reader, Office: (Word, Excel, PowerPoint,) and Illustrator (if desired)
- Internet access
- Memory sticks and three ring binders for storing hard copy information
- A dedicated work desk area
- Start learning the software programs – especially Photoshop and your digital camera

Note: Keep a record of all expenses – you will need these deductions for tax purposes.

Won't My Product Idea Be Stolen?

This is a good question. So many times someone comes to me with a product idea and the first thing they are worried about is "How do you stop others from stealing your idea?" They inevitably follow up with "Of course, I have a patent (or could get a patent) on my product."

They don't want to send their product idea to an overseas manufacturer in fear that they will be "knocked off". In fact, this fear often has crippled their progress to such an extent that they are still fearfully holding onto their idea and instead of their product sitting on the shelf they are still sitting on the fence and their idea has been frozen in time.

Fear is the most destructive of all emotions in the

product development world. Fear freezes the vision and stops it evolving. A trait of entrepreneurs is their fearlessness.

Entrepreneurs love the challenge of "going where no man dares to tread."

Protect Yourself

I do, however, agree that it pays to be cautious when exposing your product concept to others. I always have everyone I am working with on a new product sign a confidentiality agreement. That means graphic artists, product designers, manufacturers, reps (in the hiring stage), temps, employees, etc. Don't expect a retail buyer to sign a confidentiality agreement. Once you are on your "road show" and selling your product in the marketplace, your product idea is exposed to the world. Your only form of defense is to be the first one out there.

Now you can simply go online and download, for free, the legal documents you will need (i.e. Non Disclosure Agreement or Confidentiality Agreement (limits the use of confidential knowledge or materials).

• Independent Contractor Agreement (covers any

copyrightable works, ideas, discoveries, inventions, patents, products, or other information and protects your ownership along with added confidentiality clauses). This agreement should be signed by anyone you hire to assist you with any aspect of your product development. It will ensure that all work performed remains your intellectual property.

- Talent Release Form (authorizes you to make use of your talent (focus group participant) in name, likeness, portrait or pictures, voice and biographical material for publicity etc.)
- Sales Representative Contract (agreement between you and your sales representative outlining commissions, disclosure of any prior inventions that conflict with your product etc..)

Confidentiality agreements don't 100 percent guarantee that someone will not spill the beans, but you know that you have done all you can to ensure, legally and emotionally, that your product concept is protected. Then it is time to move on. To have your product concept patented is definitely worth the cost if your idea has a feature that is patentable. I have created products (i.e. talking horoscope clock) that required obtaining the necessary patents. Your trademark attorney can also patent your product.

However, most products are not able to be patented. You can copyright your design but the product may not be unique enough in its invention. For example, Caboodles™ boxes could not be patented but a special type of latch function or hinge function, if unique, could be patented. The box design can be copyrighted to protect another manufacturer from copying the design. A patent is pending until it is accepted and patents also expire – so make sure that you thoroughly research the area of patents and copyrights with your attorney. First, you may want to research the information online.

I have learned that when you sense fear it is usually a warning to protect yourself. You cannot stop the inevitable but you certainly can take all the steps necessary for survival. In the business world, naivety is a blessing and a curse. Naivety allows you to break the rules and retain your uniqueness and innovation. The downside is not knowing how to protect yourself and your idea which is one of the main reasons I have written this book. When in doubt, check with an attorney.

Homework

Print out one of every legal document for your files and become familiar with them.

- Independent Contractor Agreement
- Non Disclosure Agreement and/or Confidentiality Agreement
- Talent Release Form
- Sales Representative Contract

Research a good Patents Trademarks and Copyrights lawyer or attorney.

Developing Your Product Profile

What is Your Product Idea?

Many product ideas that have been shared with me throughout the years have originated from someone's hobby or workplace. It is often an idea that has been created to make something easier, someone's life more enjoyable, or to enhance an existing product's use.

Now it is time to mold your idea into your first product concept and, in order to do so, it is time to ask yourself some very important questions.

The answers to these questions will give you an insight into how much you know about your product already and, more importantly, what you still have to learn about your idea in order to make it a viable product.

What does your product/service do or provide?

Why would someone use it?

Why is it different from the product/services already available?

Is it an invention/unique?

Is it an enhancement?

Have you seen a similar type of product concept before and want it sell it through a different market i.e. online vs. retail. Discount stores vs. department stores.

Who would buy it?

What would someone pay for it?

How often would they use it?

What type of store/consumer would carry/use your product/service?

Would it sit on a shelf or hang on a peg in a retail store?

If it's a service – how would your consumer find it? i.e. search engines, street signage, local mailings, word of mouth, website, social media sites, etc.

What color is it? (even if it is a service – what color would you associate with it.. i.e. green for clean or vegetation, blue/white for emotion/water

What magazine would you advertise your product in?

If you don't have all the answers now, don't worry just highlight the question so that you can go back and answer it at a later date. By the time you have gone through the product development process you will not only know all the answers but will be an expert in your field.

What is Your Story?
Facts Tell and Stories Sell

Why do you think you came up with this product idea? Having a story to tell is an important element to your credibility when it comes time to sell your product idea.

People remember stories more than they do statistics and figures. Your story adds a human element to an otherwise inanimate object. The story is for selling purposes. It is not for your consumer but for your retail customers. Retail buyers are being presented with new products, improved products, tried and tested products. So what will set your product apart from the hundreds of thousands of new products ideas being presented in buyers' offices across the country? It will be your story that will set your apart. Buyers remember stories.

    Imagine that you are a buyer and have scheduled a fifteen-minute appointment with someone you have never met before. You have been convinced to meet this product developer because you respect their rep and have confidence in his or her opinion. An unknown woman enters the room and puts a new hair dryer on the table in front of you. You already purchase hair dryers from a major supplier with whom you have been doing business with for years. Their service, quality, and prices are proven entities. Why should you purchase a hair dryer from this unproven stranger? Then the woman tells her story. She has spent her life as a hair stylist for Hollywood movie stars. They have complained that hair dryers, used on a regular basis, cause dry brittle hair. She has been working with electrical engineers to invent a hair dryer that incorporates a moisturizing mist with the warm air that protects the hair while drying it. Hollywood movie stars have agreed to endorse the product and their endorsements will be featured in full page ads in leading fashion magazines.

The buyer has been told the story.

Of course this is a fictitious story – but it gives you an example of a story used to sell in a product.

Not only does your story need to explain why your product idea is unique and different but who you are too. The person behind the product is important to the buyer. Who are you? Do you have financial backing? Are you credible and reliable? Why did you come up with this idea? What is your story?

My Caboodles Story, as an example, went like this:

When I had a modeling agency in New Zealand I noticed models using fishing tackle boxes as make-up organizers. When I came to America and saw plastic fishing tackle boxes in masculine colors, I knew that all I had to do was to add a mirror, change the colors to make them more feminine, and tees would buy them to organize their make-up.

This story tells how the idea originated, gives credibility to the product, and explains who the consumer is and what she would use it for. Of course I also added my focus groups information to this story... but we will go into that later.

Write down your story and practice it over and over again until it flows naturally and easily. You must be able to tell your story in a few sentences. Your story must be honest, factual and true.

What is your story?

Your Idea Condensed Into Just One Sentence

Next, create one sentence that defines the creation of your product.

This is a key element in the early stages of development. If you cannot explain your product idea in one simple sentence it is too complicated to sell.

You have four and a half seconds to capture a consumer's attention once your product is on a retail shelf (even less on a computer screen). This four and a half seconds is what you will be working towards once your product has been prototyped and packaged. At the visionary stage it is important to simplify your thoughts and explain your product concept accurately and effectively in as few words as possible.

Take Caboodles cosmetic organizers as an example. There wasn't a cosmetic organizer box category in the stores. There were only fishing tackle boxes in the sporting goods area and cosmetic trays and cosmetic bags that could be called "similar" to my product idea in the cosmetics' area.

My first description of the product line was *"A line of cosmetic organizer boxes similar to fishing tackle boxes only in fun, feminine colors with a mirror."* Simple, a big clumsy to start with, but to the point. Every time someone asks you about your product you should be prepared with your simple one sentence explanation. You will eventually condense this sentence into a few words.

What is your sentence?

Create a Visual Of Your Product Idea

Now is the time to start putting your product idea down on paper. This is the very first stage of your product development process. There are no rules; have fun and trust your vision.

Hopefully you have installed Photoshop into your computer and have learned the basic program. Photoshop is going to be your best friend for the next few months so you had better become familiarized with it.

Three are many ways to start this project depending on what your idea is.

If it is an enhancement of an existing product you can simply take a photo of the existing product and make your changes using your Photoshop program. Of course this is 'for your eyes only' and any images you download cannot be used in the final design.

Using Caboodles as an example, I photographed my hand made cardboard working prototypes (open and closed) and placed the photos into my Photoshop program. Then I simply changed the shape of the boxes and changed the colors. Then I took photos of cosmetics and placed them digitally into the trays, added a mirror and presto, I had a whole new collection of cosmetic organizer boxes.

If it is an original concept, you can simply hand draw a rough sketch of the product, scan it into the computer and use Photoshop to manipulate it. Do not worry about the end result – remember this is just a starting point.

You can always scan a photo of a product from a book or magazine that is similar in shape and design to your vision and manipulate the image until it looks more like your product. If you are not a great artist, don't worry. Photoshop, once you have mastered the program, can transform into one. It will take a few weeks to master the program. Like anything, it just takes practice.

When you have created your first visual, duplicate this image. Create a retail shelf space in your computer (two feet, three feet and four feet wide and sixty inches tall) and start placing your products on shelves or hooks. If it needs a package or card, create something simple to hold the item. We will be working on packaging later.

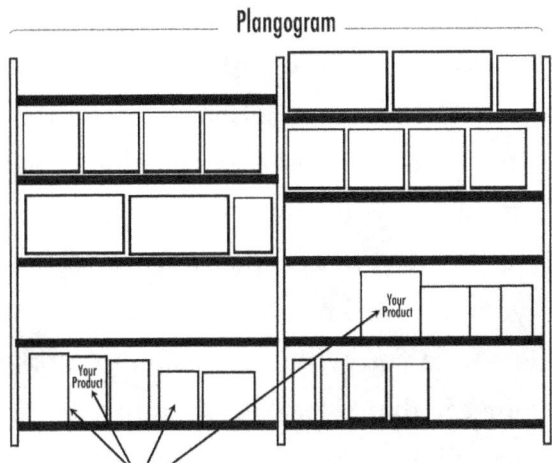
Plangogram

When you are duplicating your item you may want to try different colors and sizes of the product.

This should be fun and free flowing. You are not expected to be a graphic artist. Today's computer programs give you all the tools you need to take your product from your mind to paper. Have fun with it.

The end result you are trying to achieve is to have at least a visual of your product on paper (and on screen) that closely resembles your product idea. This illustration will be used in your first focus groups.

The image of duplicating your product onto shelves in a retails store is for your mind's eye only. Later we will work on expanding your product idea into a product line. This exercise feeds your vision and helps guide your subconscious mind in the right direction.

Whenever I create a product I visually take it from the mind to the marketplace immediately. The power of the mind is incredible. As I have mentioned before, the visual of your product line on the shelves in a retail store is crucial to the end product's success.

If you don't know where you are going, nowhere is where you will end up. For example, if you get into your car that is parked in your driveway and start driving with no particular place to go, you will end up back in your driveway. However, if you are driving to your local supermarket to pick up some groceries, you get in your car, and without even really realizing it, you find yourself pulling into the supermarket. Your weekly trips to the supermarket have been engrained into your memory. The roads, turns, and stoplights are reacted to automatically. Your subconscious mind knew the way and simply took you there. During your short trip your mind may have wandered in many different directions but you had already set your course and destination into action.

The product development process works the same way. Imagine that your product's end journey is sitting on 30,000 store shelves. With this visual engrained into your mind's eye, your subconscious mind will simply take you there. Every decision you make on the way is already programmed for success.

Follow Up:

What did you use as your initial visual to manipulate in Photoshop (photo, drawing, magazine ad, web image etc.)?

When you duplicated your image into multiple products – how much shelf space did it take?

Have you printed out copies of your first initial product concept and filed it for future focus groups?

Developing Your Packaging

What Packaging Should You Choose?

Your packaging is a billboard for your brand. It carries your product name, your logo, and your message to your consumer.

When you have multiple products on the shelf the duplication creates a billboard effect. Do an image search online for "in store planograms" and look how effective duplication is. You will notice how important the brand name is and the choice of color that represents the brand image.

Cleaning products such as "GreenWorks" look wonderful in their clear and green packaging.

Remember you are in the initial research stage so feel free to choose a number of different packaging options. You can make a more educated choice later when you have had the opportunity to talk to packaging companies and have done your consumer research.

Packaging Choices

There are various forms of packaging used in the marketplace. Now is a good time to start researching what your product needs in order for it to work on the shelf and have instant appeal to your consumer.

The type of packaging you should use obviously depends on what your product is. No matter what type of packaging your product requires, the development of your packaging is as important as the development of your product.

Making packaging prototypes is inexpensive and relatively easy. The design of the packaging, however, is not as easy. It may take you, like it took us, many attempts; shopping the stores, gathering consumer input to get it right.

The good news about the packaging is that it is very quick to produce by your manufacturer or printer. Once they have the final artwork it just takes a few weeks to have final samples; so your packaging can be ready at the last minute and still make your ship dates.

Again, you have to go back to the stores and check out other items like yours. Look at all the packaging choices. Buy the packaged items that most resemble what you want your packaging to look like. Buy one for you, one for your graphic designer and one for your, yet to be chosen, manufacturer or printer. Check out the quality of the card, box, or label. Buy the packaged product that has the card and printing quality that you want to achieve. Actual samples are better than written descriptions when you are manufacturing.

You can use these samples for costing purposes. It is easy to get a price if you have an actual sample. You can always tell the printer that it will be one inch wider and a half an inch longer but it is a good starting place.

Remember the packaging adds cost to your final product. And you will only have so much room in your pricing structure. But the wonderful thing about packaging is it is the same cost whether you have awful graphics or wonderful graphics. In some categories it is the graphics that sell the product. Take a cake of soap for example. The product is completely covered in paper. You are buying the brand, the image, the promise and the perceived value.

Look at the following packaging options and choose more than one if you are unsure which one would work for your product. You will be working on the design of your packaging later on. You are still in the research stage. And, because you are still in the research stage, you want to keep this project cost effective using paper, glue and cutout cardboard shapes.

A Simple Label

Some products require labeling only. For example; bottles, jars, lipsticks, etc.

Research your custom printed label options online. There are many to choose from; laminated labels, clear labels, foil labels, vinyl labels, permanent labels and removable labels to name a few.

You have a choice of:

• Clear Mylar™ labels (polyester or film labels) that can be printed in single or multi colors.
• A solid label printed in single or multi colors.
• A sticker – Mylar solid – printed in single or multi colors.

A label is used on bottles, pottles, jars, plastic buckets,

bins, and other exposed items where a simple label is all you need.

Hang Tags

Products that work well with hang tags are products that don't usually require a lot of packaging or if a label is not suitable. If you can simply sit your product on the self without any packaging this is idea. Products that don't require packaging are: plush toys, clothing etc.

I learned an important lesson about "to package or not to package". We made the decision to put our first Caboodles cosmetic boxes into a four color printed cardboard box. Why? Because both the retailer and I thought that we needed to explain that these fishing tackle boxes were actually cosmetic boxes. So we created big graphics on the front of the cardboard box showing the product open and filled with cosmetics. Sales were okay, we were all pleased. No one at the time knew what the potential of the new category would be so there was no way to compare sales with any other item. They were selling better than cosmetic trays, but that was no indicator as buyers had already told me that cosmetic tray sales had declined.

A year later I was at a sales meeting with all of our reps. I asked for a show of hands who thought we should take the Caboodles organizer out of the cardboard box and sell it exposed on the shelf? One lonely hand went up in the room. It was one of the few female reps in the group – one of the best reps I have ever had the pleasure of working with. Based purely on feminine intuition we made the decision right then and there – take the box out of the box and let the consumer see what they are buying.

As soon as the product was free of the packaging, it took off like wildfire with no stopping it. Sales instantly doubled, then tripled. It was lesson well learned.

Products that do not require major packaging create a billboard effect at retail. The product becomes the star. And, with four and a half seconds to catch the consumer's interest, it is a lot easier when there is a product looking at them that is instantly recognizable than a product that is hidden away in packaging. Four and a half seconds isn't long enough if the packaging doesn't scream out "Hey I am toilet tissue not paper towels!" (Am I the only one that gets these confused?)

A logo placed strategically on the product and a simple hang tag that carries your logo, brand identity and a photos of the product in use (plus the required standard information) will suffice. And a lot less expensive!

Pegged Items Require Cards

If your product belongs on a peg then chances are it requires a card. Carded items offer you a wonderful opportunity to really show your brand at retail.

The challenge is not losing the product into the card but rather have the product jump off the card.

In some cases, we had to explain what the product is especially if it was a new category and a new item. Consumers are not going down the isles looking for our product and even if they happen to give our product the four and a half second look, it takes four of those seconds to even know what they are looking at.

For one particular product our company created, we spent days and nights for months trying to create a card that would "do it all". Finally we chose a design and mocked up almost one hundred cards to hold our product sample at our first trade show. The packaging was all developed in Photoshop and printed out on glossy paper and glued to cardboard. The result looked great. Only a trained eye could tell the cards were prototypes.

A category manager from a major drug chain, whom I have known and respected for many years, stopped by our trade show booth. He liked the product (animal ears that stuck to bicycle helmets with suction cups) but said the packaging wouldn't work in drug stores, as his stores don't carry helmets and his customers would not know what the product is used for. He suggested creating a die cut around our helmet image and therefore making it instantly obvious the product is worn on a helmet.

He was right! After the show we mocked up another one hundred cards with the new die cut design and sent them out to the reps to replace the old cards.

We still hade time to change the artwork and get the disk off to our manufacturer in China before production began.

What packaging would be the most appropriate for your product?

If your product is a service – this is the time to create your "image". What color best represents your service (i.e. eco – green)?

What typeface represents your service (i.e. kids – comic style)?

What images represent your service (i.e. laundry – white, pressed)?

What emotions represent your service (i.e. babysitting – reliable, safe)?

Visualize your Consumer

When I turned my home in New Zealand into self-contained suites with three separate chalets I had a vision in mind.

I remembered staying in a wonderful cabin in Sedona, California. The owners of the resort had thought of everything their guests could possibly want down to a portable CD player complete with romantic music CDs. The atmosphere of my cabin was so romantic and inviting. So when I decided to create an accommodation business I incorporated this image into my vision.

My vision was to create a private, romantic getaway for young couples – hot tubs on private decks, open double showers, movies, romantic music, luxurious linens, cuddly bath robes and so on. It was a great success. I can't count how many marriage proposals were made and accepted at the Chalets.

Visualize your consumer and then cater to their needs.

Defining Your Consumer Target Market

Who is Your Consumer?

It is important to decide upon your target market before developing the product any further.

If your target market is babies then your packaging, price points, and marketing is going to be directed towards parents, grandparents, uncles and aunties.

If your target market is three to seven-year-olds, then you will be targeting both the child and the adult.

If your target market is eight to twelve-year-olds, then you will be targeting both the pre-teens and their parents (the ones who control the money) with an emphasis on the pre-teen consumer.

If you are targeting teens (thirteen to nineteen-year-olds) then you are targeting teens and you hope you are not targeting their parents. No teen wants anything their parent would buy.

∞

Are you targeting young married couples? Seniors?

Baby Boomers? Millennials? (now America's largest generation), Eco friendly consumers? Working couples? Parents? Etc.

Is your market female, male, gay, adult, teen? Are you sure? Who is your target market? Who therefore is your consumer?

Knowing your consumer target market is a crucial element in the development process and will be incorporated into your product design, packaging design, brand identity and advertising style.

We chose the teenage girl market as our Caboodles consumer and focus groups confirmed that we were right. Young teens in the late 1980s were just being recognized as a viable new consumer by mass retailers. Our Caboodles brand could take advantage of this new market opportunity. Teen magazines craved new products to introduce to their readers and so did the retailers.

Learn From Your Focus Groups

How Do You Define Your Consumer Market?

Is your consumer market really who you think they are? Focus groups, focus groups, and focus groups. Every product I have ever created has been consumer focused over and over again. Not only do consumer focus groups give you confirmation of your product's credibility, but the information you will gather from these focus groups will make up a major portion of your future selling materials. So don't forget to take lots of digital photos (on high resolution) and lots of notes.

Focus group are the least expensive way to get immediate reaction to your product.

Your first focus group can be held with a small group of eight to twelve participants. They can be friends, neighbors, relatives, school friends, sports teams, PTA members, church groups etc.

Choose a group of people who you think will be your end consumer (the person who would buy and/or personally use your product). Invite them to your home or your office. Supply soda and pizza (the group is kids). Give away a small gift to say thank you. Bring with you a "talent release" document giving you permission to use their photograph and comments in your sales and PR materials.

Your first focus groups will be held as soon as you have created your first "visual on paper". The earlier the better. This focus group will determine who your consumer is, what their buying habits are, if they would buy/use your product and what they would pay for your product. It is imperative during the early stage of your product's development you obtain consumer approval for your product idea. You will learn what type of store they would expect to carry your product and how often they would shop for a similar product. Use this initial focus group to find out if your idea is a viable one of if you need to go back to the drawing board.

Your second focus group will be sued to focus your logo, brand name, and product line selection. You can also use this session for packaging and promotional ideas.

Your third focus group will be held when you have an actual product and packaging/promotional samples to focus.

Do not use the same consumers every time. The more consumers you can expose to your product, the better the information. You can never run enough focus groups.

You may want the consumers to bring their favorite product or service information to the focus group session; a product that relates to the same category as your idea so you can learn from this information.

When we are focusing cosmetics or bath and body products we learn a lot about our consumer and their buying habits from their favorite items. What price they are paying for similar items, what fragrances they like, what colors, etc.

If you are not sure of your target market, run as many focus groups as you need to define the age group that will be your end consumer. If you are still getting a low percentage of people who would buy your product then take that as a warning. You may need to make some serious changes to your product idea. Look at their reasons for not purchasing your product.

This should tell you where the problem lies. Don't think that you know more than your consumer. I have made this mistake and paid dearly for it. If you are not getting over 85 percent acceptance - you do not have a product yet.

Your product will be focused continually throughout its development. Remember the more information you can obtain during the visionary stage, the more time and money it will save you in the future.

A vision is free but development costs money, and manufacturing costs and investment into materials costs even more. It is best to make as many changes as possible in the visionary stage.

Three Points of Advice At Focus Groups

Don't Be a Salesperson

Firstly, remember you are there to learn, not to sell your product. Explain your product clearly and briefly. Try to avoid the temptation to convince. A good salesperson can sell almost anything to anyone. Remember that your product has to sell itself in four and a half seconds.

I have learned this the hard way. I created a product line that I believed in 100 percent. I created the product and used focus groups to learn consumer acceptance for the product. The groups gave it less than a 50 percent acceptance rate. I chose to ignore their input believing that once they saw it on the shelf they would buy it. After all, I had always been successful; I was the expert. I had taken two brands to market successfully. Oh the ego!

Well I spent all the money I had – and borrowed what I didn't have – to take the product line to market. I licensed some products to major manufacturers. Others I manufactured myself. It was a successful sell-in. I got the product to market. My dream had, once again, come true.

Well, so I thought. I wasn't long before my

dream turned into a nightmare. It didn't sell through enough to warrant any reorders. I lost everything. But I learned a lesson I would never forget.

Leave Your Ego at the Door

Secondly, get rid of your ego. I always explain at every focus group that we learn from our mistakes. I say "Don't be kind, be honest. It is better to know what we are doing wrong at the early stage of development so we can correct it now." Every word of criticism should be joy to your ears. You can take your product to market but you can't make anybody buy it. Your product can only improve and evolve with information. Accept it and be grateful for it.

Know What Questions to Ask

Thirdly, ask the right questions. Have each participant write their name, age and sex at the top of each page. Always provide a simple two page questionnaire. Follow every question with a "why?"

For example:

Question: Do you use a cosmetic organizer box?
Answer: Yes

Question: Why?

Answer: Because it keeps my cosmetics organized and when I am not using them I can keep my box under my bed so my little sister can't use them.

This response can give you "the size of your market". If 90 percent of the consumers you focus use a product similar to yours. This gives you great statistics for your sales materials.

Negative responses also give you excellent information. Such as:

Question: Do you use a cosmetics organizer box?
Answer: No

Question: Why?
Answer: Because all the cosmetic boxes are too small to hold my cosmetics. I have lots and lots of cosmetics.

This information tells you that there may be a market for a large box. If you continue to get this response from your consumers, then you may consider adding a larger box to your product line. If however, this is an isolated case, then remember that you are selling to the masses and your product has to appeal to the majority of people most of the time (85 percent approval). You cannot afford to create a product that only appeals to a small percentage of your target market because, obviously, on a small percentage will buy it.

An example of utilizing your focus group information is:

Question: Would you purchase this cosmetic box?
Answer: Yes

Question: Why?
Answer: Because it is big enough to hold all my make up. I like the two swing back trays and the big mirror.

Take advantage of your focus group results. For example you may take a photo of this particular girl with your product. Scan the photo into your computer and under the photo write her quote.

"It is big enough to hold all my make up. I like the two swing back trays and the big mirror." Susie. Age 15

This photo immediately shows the type of consumer who uses your product, and her endorsement of the product is a powerful selling tool in your sales materials.

Some questions you will want to give a multiple choice answer. This way you can tally your responses with percentages and use this information in your sales books.

Question: How often do you buy this type of product?

Answer:
Every Six Months – 10%
Every Year – 40%
Every couple of Years – 40%
Never – 10%

This question gives you "buying habits" and also enables you to look at the potential sales volume your product could generate.

Now lets have some fun! How big is your market? For example, take your target market – lets say it is a teenage girl consumer

Number of teenage girls in the USA – 10 million
40% purchase a product yearly – 4 million per year
40% purchase a product every two years – 2 million per year
Potential yearly unit sales – 6 million units
Selling price to the retailer (wholesale price of $5) -$30 million per year
If the retailer takes a 50% margin - $60 million retail category per year.

This means that your category, based on your focus group information is a $60 million retail category. Of course, you will need a substantial number of focus group participants in order to obtain a fairly accurate statistic.

We find that fifteen hundred participants give us a good representation of our target market group. But smaller groups can still assist you in your early product development process. Just remember that one opinionated participant in the group can influence all the others. Use the collective information obtained from a number of different focus groups before you let it influence your development process.

Include some of the same generic questions at every focus group.

You can always add more questions at each focus group as your require more input.

The Power of Consumer Focus Groups

I cannot emphasis enough how important focus groups are in your product development process. For eighteen years we ran our focus groups at a high school every eight to ten weeks with over one hundred students giving their input at every session.

My daughter, Toni, upon graduating college, became my business partner and later became president of our product development company. She was a high school student when I started doing focus groups in her classroom. Toni and I shared the creative rolls in our company. She traveled the world researching trends and looking for product ideas. As a creative writer, she did most of the product and packing copy. I did the initial product development and sales calls. Toni's role also included continuing product development based on current and emerging trends and making trend presentations to our clients and retailers. We both ran focus groups to assist us in our different areas of expertise.

Our regular visits to high school classrooms offered marketing students and business development students the opportunity to work hands on with the product development and marketing process. We also shared our experiences in the marketplace.

Not every student has the opportunity to continue their education through to a college degree so it is always very rewarding to inspire young entrepreneurs and for them to know that, in this fiend, knowledge can be learned through working experience just as effectively as formal education if that option is not open to them.

Focus group information gives credibility to your product and proven acceptance by your consumer – two major elements in successfully selling your product to retailers.

If your idea is a service, your focus group questions may look like this:

Question: Do you us a cleaning service?
Answer: yes

Question: Why?
Answer: Because I am too busy to do my own housework on a regular basis

Now you learn that time is one of the reasons – but you need to find out what other reasons

Question: What do you like about your current cleaning service"
Answer: When I get home from work my home looks wonderful and it makes me happy.

Question: Why?
Answer: I am happiest when my home is in order. I feel as though my life is in order

Question: How often do you use a cleaning service?
Answer: Once a Week.

Question: Why?
Answer: I would prefer to have a service twice a week but cannot afford it.

This information is extremely valuable and has provided you with description copy for your sales materials. For example; time saving, provides peace of mind, provides a feeling of being in control of your home, elevates mood and resulting in client satisfaction.

By offering a special discount for "twice a week" service – you may also pick up extra clients.

Remember to keep all your focus group information carefully dated, documented, filed and stored in a safe place for later use.

Follow Up:

• Type out your first 2-3 page focus group questionnaire.
• Include: Name, contact information, date, age, sex.
• Attach our first computer generated initial product design to each questionnaire.
• Ensure you have enough Talent Release forms and Confidentiality Agreements for each participant
• Arrange time, date and location of focus group.
• Bring your digital camera
• Bring snacks and drinks
• Tally up all results and create a document including photos and comments of participants and keep in your "focus group" files.

Research Makes You the Expert

By the time you are ready to sell-in your product to the consumer market you will be the expert in your field. This means you will be the expert in your product's features and design, the expert in your product's category, the expert in your product's industry, and the expert in your product's consumer market.

Industry Statistics

As part of your product development process you will be researching the industry for stats, trade shows, potential retailers and distributors, trade and consumer magazines, independent sales reps, and manufacturers. It is imperative you know your industry if you are going to be successful selling your product in the marketplace.

The product and the industry go hand in hand. Entering a new industry to me is always exciting.

You start first by establishing what industry you will be selling your item to. You would have researched this when visiting retail stores and establishing what shelf area your product belong on or by researching your service online and through competitive advertising.

In order to understand the difference between the industry and the category, here is an explanation.

If your product is a new and improved body wash, the industry would be the health and beauty industry. The category would be bath and body.

When you are walking through the retail stores look at the signage above the different isles. When you find your product section look at what it is called.

Trade Magazines (i.e. Drugs Store News, Discount Store News, Chain Drug Review and MMR) break up the annual sales by industry and category. Bringing your product idea to market is your end goal. In order to do so you need to become an expert in the marketplace. This means understanding what retailers would carry your product and what industry trends are relevant to your product category. With just a click of your mouse you can read up to the minute news from the top retailers. These are your customers – research them well.

So there is no confusion, your "customer" is your retail buyer and your "consumer" is the end user of your product – the shopper who bought your product and paid for it at checkout.

Later when we are discussing the financial requirements of taking your product to market, the research you are doing now will be used to estimate your potential sales.

Search online for your type of industry. Start researching, printing, studying, downloading, filing. Through the hundreds of pages you will be highlighting the following major points:

The size of the industry.

The size of the category that relates to your product.

The growth or decline of the industry/category over the past few years.

Who are the major players in the market?

The trends in the market.

Who are your competitors?

Who are your potential retailers/customers?

What consumer magazines target your market?

What trade magazines target your product category?

Keep a list of all the websites you visit and store the information in a special bookmarks file. You need to be able to back up your statistics.

Later this information will be condensed and used in your sales collateral and on your website. As you become an expert in your product's industry... you will be able to use quick facts on social media to promote your website/product. Your social media followers will begin to rely on your information and your credibility in the marketplace will be established.

A Clear Desk, a Clear Mind

Keeping your information organized is key for the development of your vision. Your mind needs clarity of thought. A cluttered desk and a cluttered mind will clutter your mind's vision. While your conscious mind is gathering all this information your subconscious mind is sorting and filing away all the relevant information and incorporating into your visionary mind. I know that this sounds rather far fetched, but having created products continually for a lifetime, all I can say is that this is the process a creative mind goes through.

Before I begin on a new stage of development I find myself spring cleaning my work area and filing everything out of sight. Now, don't get me wrong, when I am in a creative frenzy you cannot find a space to walk on or a table to eat at. Every area is strewn with paper, materials, glue, cutting boards, products and boxes. I have been known to sleep in a bed of which two thirds is still covered with product development clutter. Information for the mind is different from the actual product development process. Information needs to be sorted and sifted through and only the most relevant information needs to be filtered through and retained. Product development is free form and flowing as you will learn in the "Developing your Product" section.

What Type of Retailers (Customers) Will Buy Your Product?

This is really a very exciting project. Once you start researching what stores carry your type of product, you will begin to understand the magnitude of the American retail industry.

I have always lived by the theory "Sell to the masses and live with the classes." There is as much work in developing a product line for a small specialty store as there is in developing a line for the thirty thousand discount and drug stores of America. The only difference is the investment capital required and the volume of sales generated.

I jokingly say, "Leonie is my name and volume is my game." The mass retail market is my area of expertise and where I have launched most of my product lines to date and where I am the most comfortable. This book, although focused towards mass market distribution, will still be helpful for creating and marketing your product no matter what area of distribution you choose; catalogs, online retailers or brick and mortar stores. These all require similar sales materials and information. The only point of difference will be in the margins they require (their profit) which, in turn, will effect both your selling price and the retail price.

The terms "margin" and "mark-up" are not the same. Margin refers to a percentage of the retail price. If the retailer doubles the wholesale price their margin is 50% of the retail price. For example if the retailer purchases your product for $5 and sells it in the store for $10 – then the retailer is making a 50% margin.

Mark-up is how much a retailer marks up a product from the wholesale cost. This same scenario would be a 100% mark-up on the wholesale price.

Mass merchandisers (Target and Wal-Mart) work off lower margins than department and specialty stores (Nordstrom) whose products are more expensive and require a higher level of customer service. Deep discount stores, such as Sams Club and Costco, work off even lower margins. Your reps can advise you what margins your retailers will be expecting to make on your product. Margins may differ for each product category.

Because each level of retailer works off different margins it makes it impossible to sell the same item to all channels. If you choose to sell mass merchandisers, then the department store market will not purchase the same product; as they cannot compete with the mass retailer's prices.

In the retail industry, margins are used in most financial analysis. It is imperative that you know what margins your retailers will be taking on your product so you know what the retail price will be. You will be doing all your cost analysis based on the retail price. I am always aiming for a retail price that gives my product a higher perceived value. (Looks as though it should cost more than it does.)

www.stores.org is one of the many websites that lists the top one hundred retails. This list also includes: company headquarters, retail sales, number of stores etc.

You can research the top five hundred online retailers in the USA and Canada through the internetretailer.com website. If this is your preferred market then this site enables you to purchase and download each company's profile, sales, etc. Another great site for gathering online shopping statistics is the Statista website.

As you research the various retailers, check out their individual websites to see if they carry similar items to your product. Keep a file on each of your potential customers. Locate their corporate headquarters (where you will be making your sales calls with your rep.) You may even be able to find out who your potential buyer is.

Purchase a wall map of the USA and mark all your potential retailers' corporate office locations. This visual assists in your mind's development process. And will assist you when it comes time to hiring your rep force.

It is imperative that you start to focus on the sales portion of your product's journey. Knowing where all your retails customers' corporate offices are will assist you with where you will need your independent sales representatives to be located. For example, Target's headquarters are in Minneapolis or very close by. It is no use having rep living in Chicago and offering to service one of your major customers in Minneapolis. When you mark your retailer's corporate location on your wall map, also mark the number of stores they have. Target has over 1800 stores in the United States and 38 distribution centers. These visuals are crucial to your journey's success.

Many retailers overlap into multiple categories. Most of the major mass merchandisers, such as Wal-Mart, Target, and Costco, are also in the tope E-retailers. Many supermarkets also carry general merchandise and so on.

Retailers generally fall into the following categories:
• Discount Stores – Wal-Mart, Target, Kmart etc.
• Drug Stores – Walgreens, Rite Aid, CVS, etc.
• E-Retailers – Amazon.com, Staples Inc, Apple Inc, Walmart.com, OfficeMax Inc., etc
• Department Stores – Gap, Staples, Office Depot, etc.
•Small independent specialty retailers –(who purchase mostly through distributors) - Mom and Pop stores, Women;'s boutiques, Cycle Stores, etc
• Wholesale Clubs – Sams Club, Price Club, Warehouse Club, etc.
• Supermarkets – Vons, Albertsons etc.

Once you have determined what retailers carry your type of item and where their headquarters are located, tally up the number of stores these retailers represent. This figure will be used later to estimate your potential sales volume

Follow Up

Who are your potential retail customers?

What type of stores could carry your product?

How many total retail customers could carry your product?

Have you made a list of where your potential retailers' headquarters are located?

Have you marked all these corporate headquarters on your USA wall map?

Have you filed all your retailer research in a separate file for future reference?

What Magazines to Research

Start researching all the trade and consumer magazines that relate to your product. This is essential information for when you are ready to begin your PR blitz. Once your product begins to ship to stores, your PR (public relations) agency will be contacting the editors of these magazines to obtain feature articles on you and your invention. Your PR agency should be located in New York where the magazines are also located and where your press events will take place. So this initial research keeps you informed on what trends are hot in your product's category and product industry and what your retail customers are focusing on.

Trade Magazines

You will be using trade magazines to educate yourself on your retail customers.

As mentioned earlier, some examples of trade magazines in the mass retail industry are Discount Store News, Drug Stores News and MMR. Do your research and read up on your particular retailer outlet. Each magazine has their own website which provides current information relating to the retail market. However, you usually have to subscribe online in order to have access to their market research.

Try and obtain at least one hard copy of each magazine. These trade magazines will become your bible. You will be familiarizing yourself with what retailers are doing in your category and what manufacturers' products are doing well, what products are failing, and what buyers are looking for. You can also find your industry's trade magazines at trade shows.

When I was first researching the retail industry in America, I had only been in the country for a few months and trade magazines were my only source of information. At first I had no idea what I was reading about. The retailers were unknown to me. I had so much to learn. But six months of studying the industry, through magazine articles and information obtained by my national rep force, gave me all the ammunition I needed to familiarize myself enough to get my product on thousands of their retail shelves.

Research your particular product's industry for their trade journals and magazines. For example, if your product idea is a new type of bicycle pump, Bicycle Retailer magazine would be an industry magazine that would be ideal for your research. Call their advertising department and request a copy. Explain that you are a potential advertiser, a manufacturer new to their industry, and want to research all the trade magazines to decide which ones you want to subscribe to and possible advertise in. You may as well get a 'rate card" with their advertising offers and programs for reference purposes later.

Follow Up:

What trade magazines relate to your product's industry?

List three key information points you learned from researching retail magazines.

Who are the editors of your chosen trade magazines who write feature articles on your type of product?

Make a point of reading your trade magazines regularly.

Consumer Magazines

You will be using consumer magazines during the research stage to familiarize yourself with your consumer (your end customer who will buy your product for their own use). Later these same consumer magazines will be used for advertising your products and create consumer awareness for your brand.

Subscribe to consumer magazines that relate best to your product category and/or your consumer market. For example, if your product is a child's toothbrush, you would be looking for parents magazines, health magazines, kids magazines, etc.

As I mentioned earlier, my expertise is in selling products to mass market retailers. Once I had perfected my blueprint I was able to take a product from my mind to the marketplace in six short months. But selling in is only half way there to financial success. In order for the products to "sell through" to the consumer I needed to create instant consumer demand for my products.

With Caboodles™ and Sassaby™ cosmetics organizer boxes I chose TEEN, Seventeen, Glamour, and YM magazines. These were my teen girl consumer's favorite magazines (based on our focus group information). When our products hit the store shelves they were supported by full page paid advertisements and editorials (free articles written by the magazine editors on "what's hot") in these magazines. With millions of dollars of merchandise on the store shelves we needed to ensure that the sixteen million teenage girls of America knew what they were and where they could buy them. Within three years of launching the cosmetic organizer category we had created of 90% teen awareness for the products and the brands. Many teen girls owned more than one Caboodles and/or a Sassaby box.

Editors are always on the search for hot new products to feature free of charge. But they won't write about your product until it is in the marketplace and their readers know where they can purchase it.

Your PR agent will be contacting these trade and consumer magazines and sending them press releases and product samples when you are ready to start shipping your product into the marketplace. If you start promoting your product too early it will only frustrate your consumer.

It will be interesting to see what the future holds for magazines in printed form. Many major magazines are going online. Newsweek who, after eighty years of print publishing has opted for an online version only. I guess the increase in digital ad revenue is driving this new trend.

Follow Up:

What three consumer magazines have you chosen that best suit your product idea?

How many consumer magazines did you find that relate to your product category?

Create a list of the editors from your chosen magazines for your PR campaign.

Create a Consumer Profile

These magazines also provide you with information on who your consumer is, what she thinks, what products she likes, and her lifestyle. Choose a person who is featured in your consumer's favorite magazine that best resembles the type of person who would use your product. If it is a cosmetic product such as lip-gloss then you may choose a top fashion model or rock star. Read about this person's personality and take notes. You will need this information later for your brand development process.

Follow Up:

Have you chosen a collection of your ideal consumer photos from your consumer magazine?

Describe his/her characteristics.

What Other Products/Services Resemble Yours?

Search for information on concepts similar to yours. Remove/print these pages and keep this information filed away for later use. Search for logo styles that you like. This information will be helpful in creating your own logo and brand name. Look at who is manufacturing these products. Keep all this information filed for future use.

Follow Up:

Have you chosen at lest five logo styles you would like for your logo?

Have you chosen at least five similar product ads that feature your type of product personality?

Researching the Competition

In the product development process, I have always believed that if you are looking over your shoulder at your competition, you are not concentrating on the path ahead. Not looking over your shoulder in the early stages of development does not mean that you aren't interested in what your competition is doing. During the actual creative process I always prefer to create a product with no outside influence. This keeps my products unique and innovative. I don't review the competitor's products until I have completed my very initial product and packaging design. This prevents my vision being influenced by products already available in the marketplace and therefore reducing what began as an innovation to a mere copy. Of course, I have suggested that you "go shopping" in the initial stages to check out where your product belongs in a store - what isle, what section, etc. But doing an in-depth study of your competition before your product idea has been developed is not advisable.

I am a great believer that armed with all the information and having done all your research, you will be a leader in your specific category and, as a leader, you will be the pioneer.

Often your new product ideas come from other categories. For example fishing tackle to cosmetics.

An industry rule is "if you don't eat your own children someone else will." If you are not constantly improving your products then your competition is doing it for you at your expense.

A single product has a shelf life of approx. eighteen months, as soon as your product is hitting the shelf you should be working on your next season's product line. After all, once your product is in store it quickly begins to age and buyers start looking for "what's new". Don't panic. Often just a color or fabric change is required to keep your product fresh and exciting – at least for a year or so

Trade Shows

Now is the time to begin to research what trade shows are available and most suitable for you to exhibit your product.

There are a number of trade shows in the mass retail industry. Here are some examples: NACDS Marketplace (National Assoc. of Chain Drug Stores), International Home and Housewares Show and The Toy Fair. Obtain a list of relevant trade shows pertaining to your type of product category along with dates, location, contact names, etc. All this information will be on the web along with the individual industry information.

Check out their websites and research other relevant shows pertaining to your type of products' industry.

Exhibiting your product line at an industry trade show is an excellent way to gauge your product's credibility in the marketplace. Your product is not only exposed to your potential retail buyers, but having your products on display and being exposed to industry suppliers, sales reps, media personnel, and your competitors will give you a fairly accurate indication of your products' acceptance in the marketplace.

We would have other exhibitors lining up at the end of the show requesting Caboodles boxes for their teenage daughters. Consumers (the general public) are not permitted to attend industry trade shows. However, there are consumer shows that buyers do not attend.

Trade magazines are also present and this is an opportunity for and your product to attract media attention. Trade magazine editors can make or break your future success. Your customers (buyers) read these trade journals and keep track of what products at the shows are "hot".

∞

Check out the next big trade show. Allow yourself at least six months to prepare – longer if you feel it necessary. Many trade shows are booked out in advance. Make a phone call and talk to the sales people and ask them if there is space available. Explain the category your product falls into and your one sentence explanation of your product line.

Depending on the size of the show, a booth space can cost between $2,500 and $10,000 or more. You are interested in the smallest space and you don't want to commit to any payment until the last possible moment. If this show is too expensive, choose a less expensive show. There are often two or three shows for each industry. Check out all their promotional opportunities available as an exhibitor. When we exhibited a new product at our first new category show we took advantage of their show guide advertising and a 6ft x 6ft x 3ft glass cabinet exhibit which was positioned in the lobby at the entranceway to the show. This space generated more traffic than our actual booth space and enticed major buyers to our booth. Our booth space 10ft x 10ft cost us $2500 plus a one-time membership fee of $2500.

Follow Up:

How many industry trade shows relate to your product category? What are they?

What are the costs to exhibit at each show?

If you could only choose one show to attend – what one would it be based on cost and exposure?

Is there space available at the show? When do you have to reserve a booth space?

Setting up Your Rep Force

Who Will Sell Your Product to The Retailer?

Hiring my sales representatives was one of the most frustrating tasks when I first created Caboodles. If only I knew then what I know now.

As my expertise is in selling large volume to mass merchandisers, the most cost effective way to set up a sales force is to use independent rep agencies. The difference between an independent representative and a company sales person is an independent rep does not work for you but has his own sales company. You pay him a percentage of sales and he pays for all the expenses incurred in selling your product to your retail customers. A company sales person is your employee and you are responsible for all his expenses, insurance, wages, commissions, etc. I have always used independent rep companies and this portion of the book covers what is involved in this process.

As your company continues to grow you may decide to hire a national sales manager who will manage the rep agencies and take over the sales calls, sales projections, and so forth. However, in the early stages no one will be able to sell the product as well as you, the visionary, the ideas person, and the product inventor.

My first experience in finding sales representation was so difficult that only sheer determination and dogged tenacity brought success. My first appointment was with a major Chicago, city based, independent rep company who had agreed to meet me at my client's office ninety minutes out of the city. My client had arranged to have a large number of corporate officers present for the big meeting. This was my moment; this meeting would establish my credibility and prove my worth to my client.

The minutes ticked by as I waited for the company representatives to appear at the conference room door. One hour later I made a call to the company to enquire if their people were delayed. Finally I was told they had "forgotten about the appointment" but they could send someone out.

It was too late. I was devastated. I realized then that I needed the reps more than they needed me.

I had only been in the country a year when I started creating Caboodles. I didn't know the name of all the states or where they were located. I just knew I had to venture out and meet with potential reps and try and convince them that Caboodles was going to a "hot new line". I felt sure that when I showed them my tattered black suitcases filled with pink and purple fishing tackle boxes filled with cosmetics they would instantly jump with joy and agree to represent the line and start scheduling appointments with all the major retailers and Caboodles would be on its way. Wrong! It wasn't that easy.

For the next two months I took planes, buses and taxis into strange cities and strange suburbs. I knocked on doors and showed my product idea to any rep who would give me a moment of his time.

One day I had appointments in five different states and ended up in New York. It was my birthday, my luggage lost, and my spirits low. I had arranged to meet a potential New York rep at the baggage claim area. I was so pleased that he had actually turned up to meet me that my lost luggage was quickly forgotten.

I told him it was my birthday. He took me to dinner and secretly ordered a small cake with a candle and sang me happy birthday. He agreed to take the line. I hired him on the spot. He has remained a good friend throughout the years.

At the end of two weeks and over twenty appointments, I had hired ten independent sales representative companies comprising of over one hundred individual sales reps who collectively covered fifty states. We were on our way.

Where to Find Your Sales Representatives

NAGMR (National Association for General Merchandise Representatives) is a good source for finding your rep force.

NAGMR is a professional association that represents leading manufacturers in the over-the-counter drug-related products, general merchandise, and food.

You can order their book which lists all the general merchandise reps by territory and by the categories they represent.

However, many of these rep companies already represent up to sixty lines that they are currently selling to the retail customers in their territory and may not want o add new lines to their current work load. They may also be selling a competitive line to yours, which would prevent you from using them.

Many of these rep companies will not be prepared to take on an unknown line from an unknown manufacturer. It is not an easy task. However, if you persevere and can convince them of your product's potential success, you may be in luck.

NAGMR has an annual general meeting. New vendors can attend this conference and exhibit their lines in the hope that they can set up their national rep force.

∞

Another good source for finding your rep force is through your particular industry's manufacturing association.

During my initial research of trying to find a rep, and full of naivety, I decided to hang out at a local drug store. I figured that if I lurked about in the cosmetics' isles for long enough eventually a local rep might appear to check on his client's merchandise. Sure enough, eventually a middle-aged man in a dark suit walked confidently up the cosmetics' isle. He looked like a rep so I approached him eagerly and asked. "Are you a manufacturer's rep?"

"Yes," he replied.

"Wonderful!" I said. "I have a product line and am looking for a rep. Could we talk?"

He took one look at the strange woman with the kiwi accent and said "I'm sorry, we are not looking to take on any more lines at the moment."

I asked for his business card and when I tried to hire him again over the phone a couple of days later, I was rejected for the second time. Three years later when many of my reps had made well of one million dollars in commission, and Caboodles had become one of the biggest teen brands at retail, I thought about this rep and wondered if he ever remembered the Kiwi lady in the isle. And if he even knew he had made the wrong decision that day.

One of my favorite quotes is "Life is about the choices you make and the chances your take."

Each rep company covers a certain area of the country. Sometimes a company covers many states. If you have done your homework and marked on the map where your major retailers' corporate offices are based, you can then begin to organize your rep territories based on this information. Check that the reps you hire live in close proximity to the major retailer's corporate offices.

You want to ensure that the rep company you choose has an already established working relationship with the retail buyer you will be selling to. The reason you are paying them a commission is because of this relationship and their knowledge of the retailer's needs and expectations.

Sometimes a combination of mass market reps and specialty industry reps is required to cover all your desired retail outlets. But I would advise setting up your mass market reps first before working on other retail levels because, as mentioned earlier, specialty stores require a higher margin and will not purchase the exact same product as mass market stores.

Often you will find your first trade show will be your opportunity for meeting collectively with your rep force. If you still have areas that require a sales rep, then trade shows are ideal for hiring. Reps are already at the show with existing lines and are walking the show looking for new hot lines to represent

What are You Looking for In a Sales Representative

As mentioned, the most important value of any sales rep is his established relationship with your retail buyers. If he is not already selling other products to the buyer within your product category, you may want to keep looking for one who does.

Once you have determined what rep companies you wish to hire to represent your line nationally you will need to have them sign an independent sales representative agreement. In your earlier research you would have already sourced this agreement and have copies in your files.

Rep companies cover from one to ten states depending on their territory. Each rep company has anywhere from one to fifteen sales reps working within their company. Some companies handle over sixty separate product lines.

How Much Do You Pay A Sales Representative?

If you choose to use independent sales reps they will work off a percentage of your sales. Commissions vary from 2% to 10%. Usually a rep will only work for 2% if your line is already established at retails and generating over $5 million plus in sales in his specific area. Reps would prefer 10% for an unproven product, but may work your line for 5-7% if they feel that your product is going to generate large sales volume within the next twelve months or so. A 7% commission is often a starting point. Commissions can be reduced once sales have been established and volume has increased to such a point that a reduction in commissions could be re negotiated (usually in the two to three year time span).

Why Do You Need A Sales Representative

The advantages of working with independent reps are many:

- You don't have to pay anything if they do not sell in your product.

- Independent contractors are responsible for their own expenses – travel, accommodation, gas, and day-to-day operating expenses.
However, you are expected to pick up the tab for their meals and entertainment during your visit. Hopefully they will arrange a dinner with your buyer.

- They have the experience and contacts that you need to sell in your product to the buyers in their territory.

- They are experts in their field and will be your information source for buyer and account information.

- Always remember the reps loyalty is first with the buyers – not you. Even though you are writing them a commission check each month, their loyalty always remains with the retail buyer. I have been working with mass retailer reps since 1987 and I have learned, through them, that manufacturers come and go, but most of their retailers remain.

Many industry reps have ben in this industry longer than the buyers and are more familiar with the manufacturers, their programs, their products, etc. The retailer orders the product through our reps – without the retailer the rep earns no money. Simple result – the retailer controls the reps' income, we simply write the check.

The rep works as your middleman between the buyer and you. He can provide all the information you need on any specific account. He will also keep you updated on a regular basis. He is your line of communication to the retailer.

Your reps are in constant contact with your buyer. He is in their office two or three times a week. You are in the buyer's office one to three times a year – if you are lucky. As you feed your rep information, he is feeding your buyer information.

Every time you communicate with your rep, remember that, in today's computer age, he may be forwarding on your information to a buyer. This is not a disloyalty to you but simply an efficient rep keeping his buyer informed. Today almost all communication is done via email both with the buyer and the rep. Many major retailer buyers are requesting you provide them with your proposal via PowerPoint presentation – complete with product photos, packaging information, prices, promotions, etc. Of course, by the time you are asked for this (which you hope you are), you will have all the information you need ready and waiting.

Let me emphasize here how important it is to use your company representative at all times as your contact for the buyers. Direct contact with the buyer (unless the buyer contacts you directly for information) is not advisable as it can put you on the spot if you are not prepared. Later, if you have formed a good working relationship with a particular buyer, you may find that direct communication is sometimes necessary. But always copy your rep on any communication so he is always kept in the loop.

Wal-Mart, however, works directly with the top management of their suppliers making this retailer a lot more challenging. Wal-Mart has a process you need to go through in order to submit new product.

I remember my first meeting with Wal-Mart back in the late 1980s. My appointment was early in the morning and I was on west coast time so it felt even earlier. I pulled into the car park in my rental van and dragged my heavy suitcases up the ramp and into the main office. I checked in with the pleasant receptionist and walked into the large open waiting area. Most retailers had plush waiting areas; soft sofas, coffee areas, luxurious carpets, and indoor plants. This was America's number one retailer and I was amazed to see rows and rows of single plastic chairs. The room was intentionally uninviting, I thought. Groups of men in dark suits were deep in conversation. Others were at the wall phones and talking in hushed voices. (pre-iphone days) As I walked towards the rows of chairs trying not to trip over my long, flowing peach skirt, I noticed a sudden hush had gone through the room. It was then that I realized I was the only woman! I could hear their thoughts as I looked at their shocked faces: "What is she doing here?" I cursed myself for not wearing a conservative black suit and a hat to hide my very blonde hair.

Sam Walton had instructed his buyers to meet with me. He had told them that we had a fishing tackle box 'for the ladies'. He was a great supporter of American made products. As I left the building thirty minutes later I couldn't hide my excitement knowing I had just sold the number one retailer in the USA – peach skirt and all!

I continued to call on Wal-Mart for many years. I always enjoyed selling this account and making presentations to their buyers.

In the sales portion of the book we will be discussing your relationship with your reps and buyers.

Follow Up:

Look at your USA wall map. What cities are your top 25 retailer corporate offices located in?

How many rep agencies have you found that call on these retailers?

Begin to mark rep information on your wall map to coincide with your retailer information.

Have you ensured that every rep agency has signed a confidentiality agreement and, if hired, an independent contractor's agreement?

How are you going to get Your Product to Market?

Usually your financial situation determines how you

will get your first product line to market. If you are, like I was at the beginning of my journey, an unproven, unknown, product developer without any investment capital, (unless you have a very wealthy great aunt who is prepared to fund you), your options may be limited. But, don't let this discourage you.

You have an added advantage over me. You now have my blueprint on how to get your product through early development for very little capital investment. You also have the internet to research every aspect of your product development process. The more you can develop your idea, the more ownership you will keep in your company. Beware of companies who offer to take over your product development, sales, and distribution. If I could do it with no experience in brand and product development, no knowledge of the US retail market, and no guide to follow, then you certainly can develop your idea into a viable branded product without having to give it all away. Go as far as you can with the development process and when you feel you have something to show a potential investor then it is time to look at your options.

Once you have gained a reputation in the product development and marketing field, finding investment capital becomes a lot easier. (I raised ten million dollars for my second branded product line and it only took two weeks!)

By having the following tasks completed you will be in an ideal position to raise some capital:

- Product name and brand name copyrighted
- Product line computer generated illustrations
- Product prototype/samples (if possible)
- Focus group analysis and statistics
- Industry statistics – size of market – potential sales volume
- Potential retail customers
- Independent Rep Companies under contract
- Marketing Plan
- Projected Sales volume

You will need a business plan to present to interested investors – download a business plan template – and incorporate all your research and development information. In a later chapter I explain in more detail the different levels of finance you will need as you go through your development process into the manufacturing, distribution, and warehousing mode.

The more you have your idea developed, the less you are required to give away. Money equals ownership – don't forget that.

During my business career, I have chosen many different financial options to get my products to market from giving an idea away (for a mere wage and gained experience) to owning my own businesses and raising venture capital when needed. I have also funded my own ventures. The longer you can wait to raise capital the more ownership in your company you will be able to retain.

Manufacturers

If you choose to have your product manufactured while maintaining the ownership of your product then you will need to research custom manufacturers. So it is back to online research and sourcing manufacturers who specialize in your type of product.

In 1986, when I first had the vision to make a fishing tackle box into a cosmetic box, I went to a store and researched all the tackle box manufacturers. The major branded products were, at that time, manufactured in the USA. Then it was a simple matter of calling the manufacturers and enquiring if they were interested in using one of their existing tools to make my product.

The first manufacturer agreed to use one of his tools (molds) for the project and I was ecstatic but later, to my great disappointment, they reneged. I didn't give up. The second manufacture initially hired me as a consultant to create the line, market and develop the brand, set up the rep force and sell the product to the retailers. Later, as I didn't have the capital required to launch a full product line myself, this manufacturer hired me as an employee and immediately took ownership of the brand and the products and invested all the capital required to create market, and sell the product. They were a highly respected manufacturer with established distribution in the sporting goods category.

As an employee of this company I single handedly generated over $50 million in sales within three years. I was solely responsible for all product development, brand development, marketing and sales. I earned a yearly salary between $28,000 and $32,000 (if I remember correctly). This was the birth of Caboodles. After three years I left this company and created my own company and continued to create, market and sell branded products. My yearly salary changed dramatically from $30,000 to $360,000 per year.

A few years later, when my daughter and I owned our own marketing consulting company, She Designs LLC, the original manufacturer hired our services as independent contractors to revitalize the Caboodles products and brand (which had suffered from a rapid decline since my departure) Our new role was to research emerging trends, product development, oversee the brand development, marketing and sales, and run regular consumer focus group for a percentage of sales. Within a few short months, and the introduction of a new and improved "Jellies" Caboodles, the products and brand took off like a wild fire - along with our new legal financial arrangement of earning an agreed upon percentage of sales.

Choosing a manufacturer who already manufactured a similar item gave us instant credibility in the marketplace. Their product quality was superior, their financial capabilities to launch a major brand were undisputed, and their established company structure enabled them to instantly incorporate the line into their already profitable business for very little initial investment. They did not, however, know the cosmetics, teen or fashion market. The company's expertise was in the sporting goods and hardware industries; very different industries from the cosmetics industry where Caboodles would soon become a major player.

Although at the time I "gave away' my product idea, I was given something that money cannot buy – hands on experience. Within the first three years we had built the brand to a multi-million dollar brand. I often say that Caboodles was my college education.

With my next venture, Sassy, I found financial partners first; they researched the manufacturer while I concentrated on the product development and marketing and sales. My partners raised the necessary capital and, as President of the new company, my responsibilities were product development, brand development, sales and marketing. Together with our reps I sold over $15 million dollars ($30 million at retail) in the first six months of operation.

The US manufacturer we chose, however, was not an expert in the field of organizer boxes and our first launch was problematic. It took another year to provide retailers with the high quality product we needed to be successful in the marketplace.

In our second year I ran a promotion with cosmetic items placed in a vacuum tray on top of the cosmetics organizers. In the third year the company hired an expert in cosmetics and we introduced Jane Cosmetics. Shortly after Jane was introduced I left the company to take, yet another, product idea to market. A couple of years later the Sassaby Company was purchased by Estee Lauder.

Sassaby gave me my MBA. I learned a lot during these years. In particular, the importance of providing quality merchandise at affordable prices.

Overseas Manufacturing

My future product lines were made in China where I could choose factories that specialized in the type of manufacturing I needed and where the prices could keep my products competitive in the marketplace.

Today more and more products are made in China. The quality has improved and the product costs are usually unbeatable. When I first introduced Caboodles into the marketplace retailers were very supportive of American made products; in the early 1990s both retailers and suppliers began to source products overseas.

There is a trend now to bring manufacturing back to America as we see in the car manufacturing industry. So check out your options. Remember that, although you may achieve a better manufacturing price for your product in China, you will have extra shipping costs and a longer shipping window to deal with.

Finding the *right* manufacturer to produce your product idea is key.

Sourcing Your Product

Sourcing your product means finding out how and by whom your product can be made or purchased. Check out similar products in the stores and check their packaging for manufacturing information – made in China, etc.

How many different components make up your product? Research who makes these components and what country specializes in manufacturing them.

Do your research online. Check out manufacturers' Associations. Ask questions. Talk to manufacturers.

At this stage you are only doing research and collecting information. We will be talking about manufacturing your product in detail in a later chapter.

Follow Up:

Do you have a list of at least three manufacturers or suppliers who specialize n making your type of product? Who are they?

Where are they located?

Does your product require sourcing a number of

different suppliers? For example: plastic molded parts, voice chip components, printed labels. What are they?

Licensing Your Product

If you have an innovative idea that you feel another company may want to license from you, this may be an option. It takes away the pressure of you having to manufacture, market, and distribute the product yourself.

You will still need to develop your product idea to a stage that is perceived as viable and profitable to a potentially interested company.

I would suggest taking your product idea through to a sample or prototype stage and compiling all the necessary industry, category, and consumer focus group information before attempting to license your idea.

Selling you idea as a license to a major company is as difficult as selling your idea to a retailer and involves the same amount of work and tenacity.

If this is the avenue you are interested in pursuing set up an appointment with a licensing agent and discuss your product's licensing potential with him. Don't forget to use your confidentiality agreement. Have everyone you are meeting with sign on the dotted line. Protect yourself.

Do your research into companies that you feel may be interested in licensing your product idea. Also research what royalty fees are usually paid in your specific category. Be informed.

You may be able to approach these companies directly, but it usually difficult to license a product idea to a major company without an approved licensing agent or an earned reputation in the industry.

I have successfully chosen this path in the past with a product line that covered many different product categories (games, toys, calendars, and clocks). I approached a number of different manufacturing companies that specialized in each product category and was successful in licensing each product for an agreed upon licensing fee.

Some companies will give you an upfront payment of a few thousand dollars against future earnings.

The term of the licensing agreement can be anywhere from one to three years with a renewal option at the end of the term.

Licensing fees can range from 5% to 10%. My calendar earned a 10% fee and was for a one year term (which was renewed after my calendar succeeded in being in their top 30% best sellers – yeah!)

The other categories were licensed for three years and earned a 7% licensing fee.

You can research your particular industry for a licensing agent to contact viable companies on your behalf. The agent will obviously earn a percentage of your royalties (licensing income) if he is successful in licensing your product for you. Licensing your product does take away your control. You will not have any control over marketing and sales and may not even have control over the final design of your product. Manufacturers have hundreds of products they introduce every year and yours may get lost in the shuffle. However, this is a viable option and takes away a lot of the financial risk of launching a new product. It also gets your product on the retail shelf which, after all, is your desired end result.

Follow Up:

If you are interested in licensing our product idea, what potential licensors have you found? Who are they?

What royalty would they pay (based on industry standards)?

Have you researched potential licensing agents who specialize in your product's category? Who are they?

What percentage would these licensing agents charge you for licensing your product? Are there any hidden costs, fees etc.?

What advance against royalties could you expect to receive, if any?

Have you got signed confidentiality agreements with all the licensing agents you have discussed your product with?

Creating Your Brand

A Product's Life is Limited, A Brand Lasts a Lifetime

Often new product developers are under the illusion that a product invention will make them rich and famous. A product invention just opens the door of opportunity.

A product line (or category) captures real estate on the shelves and provides you and your company credibility and value.

A successful brand, once matured, can make you rich and famous. You cannot continue to develop your product without first developing your brand. The brand is going to determine the personality of the product and the packaging.

Creating the brand is one of the most exciting elements of product development. It is also your most valuable asset.

I remember during the early stages of developing the cosmetic organizer product line and choosing the name "Caboodles ' as the brand. I was feeling rather intimidated by the size and power of

America having just arrived from New Zealand with the population of four million. I had never heard of a Target or a Wal-Mart store. My marketing background consisted of creating and promoting my "Rastus Rabbit and Co" puppet show, creating and establishing a small modeling agency, running a few beauty pageants, and working as a panelist on a New Zealand television talk show "Beauty and the Beast" (a Dear Abby type show). Not the qualifications needed to create, market and sell my product idea to the marketplace in America.

I decided to go out and find a marketing book. I visited a local bookstore in San Diego and was a little overwhelmed by all the marketing titles. I chose a few and headed home to learn. They were full of the three "Ps" of marketing (product, price and promotion) and other terminologies that really didn't help very much. I was looking for the "How to market and sell my product" book. I turned to a page about brand names – finally something I could relate to. I read how a brand name can hurt a product line more than it can help one. Don't use silly names, it said. I looked at my name, Caboodles. I shut the book. I liked my "silly name". In this case my naively was my blessing.

A brand enables you to continue creating products and market and sell them under the same umbrella. A single item or a single product is almost impossible to sell to the mass market retailers. An item has such a short life span and cannot gain momentum. In order to be successful at retail your first product line will be tested in a few select stores. If it is successful (has a good sell through) then the retailer may choose to planogram the items into their everyday shelf space. This shelf space (planogram) is usually only changed once or twice a year; which means that your item has to general enough sales for the retailer to earn his space on the shelf. Every major retailer has a planogram of their stores. A planogram is a schematic drawing or visual plan that designates the placement of products on a retail store's shelves and displays. Some retailers divide their stores into three or four different schematics based on where the store is located and the size of the store. This means that they may have three or four different planograms based on these scenarios. The planograms are usually updated once a year.

By creating a brand and having a selection of products within this brand you can be continually updating your products and adding new items and new categories to your brand and therefore increasing sales and adding value to your company.

The Value of Your Brand

Your brand adds value to your product line. A retailer's private label is usually sold at a lower price than the branded items in your store. Brands cost money to develop and advertise. The retailer is aware of this and will accept the extra costs of purchasing a branded product from a supplier for a slightly higher price than he would pay for bringing in the item directly from overseas.

Expanding Your Idea Into a Product Line

Think of your original product idea. Can you offer this product in a range of colors (preferably three)? Can you make a cheaper version and a more expensive version (three different price points)?

If it is a body moisturizer, why not create a whole line of bath and body products?

If it is a screwdriver, why not create other tools with the same innovation?

If it is a new mirror concept, why not create different sizes and different uses? One for the countertop, one for the shower, one for school locker - all utilizing your unique product idea.

If it is a new concept of facial tissues, why not create different sizes, different packaging designs?

Later you can introduce an "updated" line of products under the same brand or license.

If it is a service how can you turn the service into your brand? My brother, Bernard, in New Zealand owns a footpath signage service. He has called his company/brand "Footpath and Beyond". He provides many different designs and sizes of signs, but specializes in footpath signs.

Your brand name, once established, is now an asset and can be licensed to another manufacturer to manufacture and distribute a line of completely different products that appeal to your brand's targeted consumer.

What is Your Brand Personality?

To me this is one of the most enjoyable tasks of brand development and the most important. Creating your brand is a key element in your product's success.

What is a brand and how is it different from your product? A product is an actual object and a brand is an identity. A brand is like a large canopy covering a multitude of different products. A brand allows you to create many different products in many different categories. A brand gathers value with age; a product loses value with age.

The easiest way to create a brand personality is to look objectively at your product idea and ask these questions:

Is it a serious product or a fun product?

Is it targeted to males or females – or both?

What age is your consumer target market?

What are the personality traits of your brand? Refer back to your "Consumer Magazine" section. What are the personality traits of the "consumer" you chose who would best represent your product? Look at the adjectives you wrote down. What are your brand's adjectives?

Once you have decided on your brand's personality then create the one sentence that best describes your brand using the key adjectives on your list. Avoid the words innovative and new. Everyone thinks their product is innovative and new.

What is your one sentence?

You will also need to describe what type of products you will be creating under this brand image – keep these very general, not specific. The more general you can be, the more value you will be adding to your brand in the future. A specific description only limits your ability to add other product lines in the future. An example would be:

"A brand of lifestyle products that allows teens to express themselves"

Describe your brand's products?

Giving Your Brand Its Name

Now we are at the point when you need to create a name for your brand. This is not the product name, but the brand name. The more generic the name the more categories can be added.

When I came up with the name "Caboodles" I was sitting in my bathtub reading a huge Oxford English Dictionary. I wanted a "C" word. I came across "Caboodles" which had the definition; "a collection or clutter of things". How perfect, I thought, for an organizer box. Hence the name was born. At that time I was searching for a product name, not a brand name. However, the product ended up being the brand name with other product categories later falling under the Caboodles umbrella.

I knew the name needed to be colorful if it was to appeal to my target audience – teens. I had arranged to meet with the owner of the manufacturing company who had agreed to finance and manufacture the products. We visited a local discount store where I chose four brightly colored plastic hair dryers in peach, yellow, pink and purple. As we were checking out, the sales clerk asked us why we were purchasing so many hairdryers.

I responded, "We are using these colors for Caboodles".

She said. "What is Caboodles?" It was the first time I had heard my new "brand name" spoken by a stranger. It was exciting.

Another brand name I created was "Sassaby™" (a South African antelope). The brand name inspired a bright African/animal style logo and graphics.

You can use a combination of words or letters to create your own name. Make sure that this name is acceptable in all languages. The brand "Osco" having the same pronunciation as the Spanish word "asco" (oss-ko) means "nausea" or "disgust". This was a problem with the growing Hispanic market in Southern California and Nevada. Luckily the brand was later changed during a re-launch of the popular American drug stores.

Another brand we created was "Oh Baby" a line of fabric and plastic infant organizers.

So how do you find the right word (one that is not already taken)? Purchase the biggest dictionary you can find.

Review your brand personality. Is it feminine and soft? Look at the words beginning with Cs and Ss and curvy letters. Is your brand solid, strong, and masculine? Look at the words beginning with sharp letters such as Ns, Ts, and Ks.

You only have four and a half seconds to sell your product at store level. The brand name has to have instant appeal and be instantly read and understood.

Another project that can assist you with developing your brand name is to create a page on your computer using Photoshop. Scan in an ad that you have chosen from a consumer magazine that is of a similar product to you. Replace their product with yours. Replace their logo with your name. You can even at this early stage, take another company's logo style and incorporate this style into your name.

Look at the page; does your name work with your product? Does it best describe your brand personality?

Your Domain Name Should Match Your Brand Name

Don't forget that it may be difficult to find a name that is still available for your domain name so before naming your website, or brand, or business, check out if the brand name you want is still available; if not, it may not be too expensive to buy the domain name from the current owner. It is important to have your domain name match your brand name. Do your research.

Once you have chosen the perfect word it is time to have a copyright attorney do a search. It is always good to have one or two back up words in case your first choice is not available. Each search costs approximately $100. You can, of course, do a search online yourself before spending your hard earned cash on a professional search. Look for a good copyright/patent attorney on the web who can give you an estimate for a search and give you advice on registering your name. However, it is advisable to wait until you have your logo or "mark" to register with the name if you find it is available.

Follow Up:

What are your favorite brand name choices?

What is your first choice of Brand Name? Why?

How many different products can you imagine you could create with this same brand name?

List the products?

Have you done a quick search online to see if this name is available? Is it?

Have you created Photoshop page with your product wearing its new brand name? Does it suit?

Write ten descriptive words that come to mind when you read your brand name.

Do these descriptive words relate to your product/s?

Have you located your copyright/patent attorney? What are the costs involved?

Creating the Logo (Developing Your Mark)

Creating your logo is one area that your money will be well spent providing you find the right graphic artist. When you research graphic artists look at the work they have done and the logos they have created. I now use fiverr.com for a lot of my graphics. This website offers experts in many creative field for such affordable prices. I have had fiverr.com create many Facebook headers, Twitter headers, website headers, book covers, book trailers, logos, and more.

    Choose a logo style you particularly like and give him/her your brand personality description and your one sentence description of your product, your company and your brand. Provide them with any ads or photos that best represent your brand. The more information you can provide the artist – the better the end result.

    I like working with fiverr.com because you agree on a price upfront and the designer will give you a deadline to complete the job It is a very fast turnaround. You can always pay for two or three different logo styles to give you options.

As mentioned, it is better to wait until you have your logo before you copyright your name. This way you can copyright your mark also. However, before you spend money on graphic artists, make sure you have done a pretty thorough search yourself to ensure your chosen name is not being used in the categories you want to register it in.

Remember your brand name is only your biggest asset if you actually *own* it. To copyright your brand name and logo is money worth spending.

You get charged for every category you register your brand. Now you can also do a worldwide copyright. Back in the late 80s you had to register your name and mark in each country individually – at a great cost. Check with your copyright/patent attorney as to the options available to you.

As you begin to add other product categories to your brand, you will need to register your brand name in these categories also.

Follow Up:

Have you done your final search to see if your brand name is available? If so, it is time to contact your copyright/patent attorney to protect your name. Keep a second and third choice available in case he finds your chosen name already taken.

Have you done a search for a graphic artist who has a good reputation for designing logos. Fiverr.com artists have customer feedback you can read before committing to any particular graphic designer.

Make sure you add ™ to your logo – later you can add a ® for a registered mark.

Expanding Your Vision

Don't forget real estate at retail is your second biggest asset when selling your brand or your company in the future.

Is Your Product Idea Unique Enough to Create a Category?

If your product idea is unique enough that no other product exists in the marketplace, chances are you may also be fortunate enough to be creating a new category. A new category is worth gold in the marketplace. It provides retailers with extra sales; to a retailer, a new category means they are not taking away sales from another product.

For example if you have a new and improved lipstick you want to sell them, they know that there are only so many lipstick sales out there. And your product will be taking away sales from another lipstick product that they are already selling. Of course, you can argue that your lipstick will sell more than their existing lipstick on the shelf, and, might even encourage more people to wear lipstick. But the retailer buyer will still see your product as "just another lipstick" and he only has so much space on his shelves for lipstick, and if he purchases your lipstick he will have to take someone else's lipstick out to put yours in.

Caboodles cosmetic organizer boxes created a new category at retail. It was also one of the first teen brands to be introduced at retail. Because there was no "home" for boxes in cosmetics, our product was put on promotional "end caps" (end of isles). Once the product was a proven success, planogram space was developed especially for this category. The retailer had to take space from an existing tired category in order to create a new space. Caboodles went from a 5 shelves x 2 foot space to a 4ft space to an 8ft space and during Back to School and Holiday seasons Caboodles were often stacked on top of planograms running whole isles.

If your product idea creates a new category at retail this will be one of your strongest selling points and needs to be incorporated into your sales materials.

A new category can also be more difficult to introduce initially because the buyer has no history to refer to. That makes your industry and category research essential. You will be the expert in this new category and before you meet with your first rep and your first buyer you will be armed with the information showing the size of the industry the category relates to, the potential of the new category, the number of consumers that relate to this category, the potential volume that could be generated from this new category, etc.

Creating Your Product Line

So now you have a brand personality, a name and a logo. You even have a rough visual of your product line.

Lets use Caboodles as another example. I started with a vision of a single fishing tackle box with two swing-out trays. When we created the category we called it "the cosmetic organizer box category."

When we first created the product line we chose seven fishing tackle boxes in seven different sizes, five different colors and five different price points ranging from $2.99 to $24.99.

The best seller was the one tray at $9.99. Not the one I had originally visualized which sold at a higher retail.

The following year we introduced three new organizer boxes with rounded corners and swing back mirrors. Within a few years the brand expanded into a large selection of cosmetic organizers, a full line of cosmetic bags, a collection of bath and body products and a leading line of cosmetics.

New products were introduced every year and new categories were added – all under the brand name of Caboodles giving the owner of the brand a valuable asset.

Creating a product line means that you are creating a bigger visual at store level. One lonely product sitting on the shelf can be overlooked in four and a half seconds. A group of products create an instant billboard and has much more visual impact at store level.

So back to our product line and back to your original vision of your product. Has your vision grown with the information you have been feeding it? Have your focus groups influenced your vision based on the consumer response? Or has your vision remained constant in its concept design based on consumer acceptance?

Extending Your Product Idea Into a Product Line

The first stage is simply taking your original product and asking the following questions:

Can I offer this item for different prices? What prices?

Can I offer this item in different sizes? What sizes?

Can I offer this item in different colors? What colors?

Can I create other items within the same category using the same features/uniqueness as my original product idea? What items?

How many items can I create using the same idea?

How Many Products Should you Introduce?

You will need to do some research to answer this question.

Will your product be carded and sold on a peg? Or will your product be packaged and sit on a shelf? What type of packaging will your use?

How many products will fit on a retail peg?

How many pegs will fit in a two-foot section, four-foot section in a retail store? Or if your product will be sold sitting on a shelf, how many products will fit in a one-foot, two-foot, three-foot and four-foot section?

Now you know how important it was to visit a retail store at the early stages of your product development process. You may have to visit a selection of stores. Choose stores that would purchase your product. Check out their shelf space, how many products other manufacturers offer within their lines? How many different styles and price points are there in the competitors' product lines?

Remember, the retail buyer is the expert. He

knows what is selling. With today's computer age the buyer gets instant feedback as to his product sales at the touch of his computer. Every manufacturer's product sitting on his shelves have already gone through the test stage and have earned their space on the shelf.

There is both promotional space and planogram space in the stores. The buyers have more flexibility with their promotional space as it can be changed on a regular basis. Unlike their planograms which are usually set in stone for a year. The buyer may choose to increase shelf space in a promotional area if products are selling well. In order to do so he has to reduce another category. There is only so much shelf space in the store.

This is another reason why you have done so much research into your product category. If you know your category is growing in leaps and bounds, so do the retailers. They may be looking for new items to add to the category. If, however, you find that your category is doing poorly you have an opportunity to revitalize the category with your innovation (such as the decline in the cosmetics tray business as we introduced Caboodles cosmetic boxes). A declining category is difficult to introduce new items into unless it is totally innovative.

Take the hosiery business. When we researched this industry twenty years ago it had declined 50%. Teens and many young adults didn't wear pantyhose anymore. This opened up a new category of self-tanning products – consumers preferred to have bare legs. Bare legs need to look good. Leggs™ would have been wise to package fake hose (self tanning lotion) in their wonderful egg-shaped packaging instead of allowing new manufacturers to enter this new market.

Look again at the retail price points. Look at the size of the packaging. See how the manufacturers designed their product to enable as many products as possible to fit on the shelves. Shelf products have to be able to be stacked on top of each other. Carded products have to fit on pegs and in the spaces provided.

It is a good time to go back to your computer and start creating images of a collection of products that work effectively on the shelf. Even add the retail price to each product so that you are beginning to document in your mind he product line at retail.

The products can be very rough at this early stage.

Taking Your Product from Paper To Prototype

Now you can take your product idea from a rough drawing to an actual product.

This is where your Photoshop skills will be needed. If you have not mastered this program yet you will have to get some help from a product designer.

It really depends on what type of product you are creating as to what tools you will need in the product development stage.

This stage fuels your creative vision. You will be making your first three dimensional product complete with packaging.

Having a product that your focus groups can actually touch and feel is imperative in the success of your product. You can make changes now that don't cost a penny. Once you get into factory samples and finished product you don't want to be making changes.

Mock Ups, Prototypes, and Samples

The following mock-ups, prototypes, and samples are

all part of the product development process. Depending on how finished they appear depends on what you can use them for.

The will be used in your focus groups to make sure that you are still on the right track. Remember you are looking for over 85% acceptance for your idea. So the better your samples are the better you will get an accurate read. These samples are also for costing purposes. You can get fairly accurate manufactured costs based on good samples/mock-ups.

You will be keeping your product photos updated – replacing your rough first illustrations with these more accurate depictions of your product idea. These photos and samples will also help with setting up your rep force. It is difficult to convince a major sales company to take on your product if you only have a vision in your mind. Mock up packaging will have your new brand logo and brand personality which starts to bring your whole product line together. This is a very rewarding and exciting time for a product developer. You should be able to do most of this work yourself except for the actual samples, which would be provided by your chosen factory. Keep costs to a minimum. If your product samples, packaging, or prototypes need a professional touch to get to this stage then research a good product/and /or graphic designer to assist you. Make sure he signs an independent contractors agreement so that all the work remains your intellectual property.

Take into consideration that you don't have a saleable product or a brand yet and are still in the development stage. But your vision is beginning to take form and you are well on your way to having a viable product to sell.

Here is a brief description of what your next stage of product development requires.

- Mock-ups – Cardboard packaging, stickers and labels that have been computer generated to resemble the finished product.
- Prototypes – Hand-made products out of wood or plastic which are painted to resemble the final product. These are not the final prototypes (i.e. machined prototypes constructed using CAD/CAM software or rapid prototypes (layered manufacturing using three dimensional CAD drawings)
- Sample products – Actual manufactured products made in limited quantities (i.e. fabric samples).

Products Best Suited For Mock-up Samples

In order to show your brand to its best advantage it is idea to mock up packaging and, if appropriate, in-store display units (i.e. counter top display, floor stand display, etc.)

A mock-up sample is computer generated and then printed out and glued to cards and cardboard display boxes.

I would suggest visiting a store and see if they have any old display units that are being destroyed. (These units are disposed of when their promotional period expires). If you can't get an actual display unit then take the exact dimensions and create your own.

Your product samples look so much more impressive when they are housed in a branded display box.

Remember, if you are using a third party to work with you during the product development process make sure they have signed a contract that ensures all of the work (designs) belong to you.

Products Best Suited For Prototype Samples

These products often require a mold or molds to be made (i.e. plastic buckets, cosmetic cases, toys, cosmetic containers, bottles, jars, etc.) They are usually made out of plastic or metal materials.

A mold made domestically in the United States is more expensive than a mold made overseas such as in China. Some products require more than one mold. A plastic cosmetic box requires multiple molds as there are a lot of individual plastic parts that make up the product (i.e. outer shells, trays, latch, etc.) The bigger the product, the more expensive the mold. A small plastic lipstick case mold can be made for a few thousand dollars whereas a large molds can cost tens of thousands of dollars – now is a good time to get mold quotes from selected custom manufacturers. Keep yourself protected with confidentiality agreements.

It is cost effective and recommended to have a hand-made prototype made first. It will also enable you to get an initial cost estimate for the mold and a per-unit cost based on quantities.

You have a number of choices when it comes to prototypes. For my Caboodles boxes I would first create a cardboard working model just so I could look at the size and shape. Then I would have a solid (non working) prototype created so I could decide on the design of the final product. Finally I would have a working prototype created.

Laser technology available today is quite phenomenal. Final design/engineer (CAD/CAM) drawings can be loaded into a computer program and a prototype can be made directly from state of the art computer systems. Called CNC machining and RP machine processes. As mold costs for large injection molded products are so expensive, all the kinks can be worked out in the prototype stage. Changing a final mold that is already in production is not recommended.

You can source Prototype manufacturers online when you are ready to have your final prototypes made prior to production. These manufacturers offer a wide range of prototype materials from plastic, acrylic, ceramic, laser and steel to automotive, electronic, polystyrene, optical and much more....

Before you can get a mold made, you will have to go through an approval process for both the engineering drawings and the final parts drawings for the mold maker.

Remember that when a factory gives you a per-unit cost it may not include the mold cost. Some factories, providing the volume is going to be substantial enough, will provide a small mold free of charge in order to get the business. However, if you are just starting out, you will most likely have to pay for the mold costs up front. Some manufacturers will amortize the mold costs (including these costs in your per-unit cost) until the mold has been paid off.

In my early days of product development, before Photoshop, I used to create all the cosmetic organizer boxes out of cardboard. Complete with swing back trays and mirrors. All the organization was created with strips of cardboard, sticky tape, and glue. I still like to begin with this process, but today I can take photos of the cardboard prototypes and manipulate the design in the computer to resemble the final product.

Once we have taken the product to this stage, a product designer is hired to add the final design elements to the product and an engineer takes this information to complete the engineers' drawings - which are required to create the actual mold parts.

Once a working prototype is made and approved, per unit product costs can be established.

The mold can take 90 to 120 days to create. Then sample products are tested and approved before production can commence. The whole process from concept (cardboard prototype) to final product can take up to nine months. A smaller item with a less complicated mold can be done much more quickly.

Having a prototype made is essential to your product's success. A computer generated illustration can be used for the initial focus groups and for sales materials but you cannot sell in your product or get an accurate read as to how your consumer or customer (buyer) will accept your product without a working prototype.

If you final product has a lot of moving parts it may be a good idea to have a non-working, less expensive solid prototype made first so you can approve the design before you invest in the next stage.

Never, never, never get a mold made without a prototype.

Review:

- Computer generated drawing of your product
- Product designer's drawing of your product
- Solid prototype - showing design element
- Engineers drawings of your product
- Working prototype of your product
- Final parts drawings for the mold makers
- Mold made

- Sample products made
- Final production

If the mold you are making is small you may be able to make a rough prototype yourself and provide enough information for the factory to proceed to engineering drawings. For example when I created bottle shapes for the Caboodles bath and body product line, I used a children's molding material I purchased in a local stationery store. It was soft, pliable, and easy to work with. I hand molded the shapes of the bottles and when they had hardened they were sent to the factory in China for prototyping.

The factory used these rough hand-made prototypes to develop the required drawings for mold production. Drawings were approved and real prototypes developed before molds were made.

I was also able to photograph these crude hand-made molds and manipulate them in the computer to create a resemblance of the final product. In order to create the actual ingredients (clear glittery liquid) inside the bottles we mixed up liquids and glitter and photographed them in clear bottles and simply cut and pasted the images onto our mock up bottles graphics. Our logo was superimposed over the new bottle images along with the product name and presto- our whole new line of products complete with bottle shapes, ingredients, and brand image came to fruition. These images and the hand made prototypes were used in focus groups with teens for initial feedback and provided to our factory for early costing purposes.

Real Product Samples

Real product samples don't require a mold and are usually made out of some sort of fabric (i.e. soft toys, clothing, backpacks, etc.) This is the easiest and quickly product to take to market as it does not require a mold and sample fabrics can be used to create your product sample.

You will still need a good illustration of the product. The manufacturer can work with a color illustration, a sample of the fabric you want to use, and the product's dimensions. The better the illustration you send to the manufacturer, the better the sample.

With one product line we used animal ears and noses taken from existing soft animal products and made the changes in Photoshop to resemble our final product concept: Helmet Toppers.

Our contracted factories in China were very creative and they assisted us with the initial product designs. Samples were made quickly for us to approve. Some products required more changes than others. The factory would email us photos of the product samples so we could make any required changes before shipping the finished samples.

Our products were made out of plush and vinyl fabrics. It is a lot less complicated and a lot less expensive to create product samples when fabric is used. Often the exact color or specific type of fabric is not available and has to be ordered (thirty day lead time and expensive) so a substitute fabric is used which is similar in color and appearance.

Product samples can be made very quickly (within a week or two), changes can be made, and final samples that resemble the finished product can be used very early in the product development process.

You will also be able to get a fairly accurate per unit cost once you have approved the sample and have decided on the fabric that will be used in the final product. Do not agree on any price quote you receive until you have done your product pricing analysis. (See pricing your product section).

Costing is based on volume. The more units you will be ordering, the cheaper the per-unit cost is. It is a good idea to get costs based on three different volumes. We will talk about how many products you will be selling in the sales projections section of this book.

This is Only Early Days Yet – Have Fun

Be creative in the early stage of your product's development. The more you can do to create a three dimensional model of your product idea, the cheaper it is for you and the easier it is for your manufacturer to understand what you require.

It is also easier for a manufacturer to give you an initial per-unit cost and, if the product requires, an initial mold cost of you have a three-dimensional prototype of your product idea.

Made this project fun. It may take you many attempts, using different materials, to create something that even closely resembles your product idea. Don't worry, once you have photographed your hand made prototype, your Photoshop program can transform it into your dream product. If you feel you simply can't create your own three-dimensional model, get professional assistance.

Some products require an expert trained in product design to give it that extra something that an amateur product developer can't achieve. Remember that once a mold has been made you cannot make any changes. (You can, but you won't want to as it is usually cost prohibitive). Look at your working prototype and call in a product designer if you are not happy with the result. (If you haven't done so already). Never let your ego get in the way of product development.

At each stage of your product's development you should be running focus groups. As soon as you have a three-dimensional model of your product get some feed back. The earlier the change, the cheaper the change will be.

The Size of Your Product

One mistake I constantly made was making my products too big. For some reason, in the early stages of development, my mind's eye could not create a product that was small enough. It was almost as though the product had its own ego. Many of our products are designed for the teen girl market and in this market the products have to have "cute appeal". Cute usually means small. Our boxes have to look small on the outside and big on the inside. When I create the first three-dimensional prototypes the product size looks good, but when it gets to the solid prototype I have to ensure that the product's size is perfect.

In order to ensure that your product ends up the size you want, purchase a product similar in size to what you want your product to be and keep to the same dimensions in your early product design. Size is an important element of your product's success.

Size also relates to the price point (what it will sell for in the store). Your product must always have a higher perceived value – looks as though it costs more than it does.

Packaging Design

As you are working on your product samples or prototypes you should be working on your packaging design. Check out www.fiverr.com - and search for product package design. There are so many package designers to choose from for very, very affordable prices.

Decide on the type and size of your packaging. You have already done your research and should have a clear indication of what type or types you wan to mock up.

Start making prototypes yourself using your graphics printed onto glossy paper and glued to cardboard. If you are working with a package designer make sure you provide them with packaging samples of what you like, colors, etc.

Choose your colors that will represent your brand. Think about female vs. male colors. Thank about the age group that will be buying your product. What did you learn about colors in your focus groups? What did you learn about packaging in your focus groups? Incorporate all this information into your packaging development process.

Information Needed On Your Packaging

You have to provide certain information with your product no matter what type of packaging you choose:

- Your logo
- Your product name and model/item number
- A brief description of the product
- Any safety warning (if applicable)
- Made in China (if applicable)
- All new material (if applicable)
- Instructions on how to use the product (if applicable)
- Your brand name – a registered trademark
- Your web address
- UPC code

Remember the four and a half second rule. Make multiple cards, put your product on them and pin them on a large board (create your own in-store environment). Or put your boxes on a shelf unit. Or attach your hang-tags to your products or your labels on the bottles or jars and sit them on the shelves.

We used actual store fixtures – end caps, three-foot shelf units, side-kicks, etc. to display our products during their development stage. What looks great on an individual card may not work when the image is multiplied many times.

Use these boards and shelf units at your next focus group. Don't tell the focus group what the product is. Give them a moment to look and then ask them "What is this product?" If they have to think about it you have lost your sale. It has to have instant recognition. You will not be there in every store sitting like a little elf on the shelf giving your sales pitch. Your packaging or your product has to do your sales pitch for you. Keep going back to the drawing board until you get it right.

If you are using a graphic artist to create your packaging make sure that packaging is his area of expertise. Many graphic artists think they can create anything that requires graphics – wrong. Packaging is an area unto itself. Mass market (self selling) packaging is the most difficult to create.

It is also important to keep all your brand images consistent. If you are using purple and yellow as your two major colors – then keep these colors consistent throughout all your packaging. You are trying to create a billboard effect at retail. This billboard is your brand image. Your logo remains consistent. Don't confuse the consumer with too much information or too many colors.

Once you have decided on the type of packaging, the quality of the packaging, how many colors, and the size of the packaging you can finalize the per unit cost. Again, get three costs based on volume.

Continue to use your focus groups. The graphics can be changed prior to production without affecting the cost.

POP In-Store Display Vehicles

There are a number of different point-of-purchase (POP) display units in which you can merchandise your product at retail.

You, as the supplier, have to pay for the display and amortize the cost of the display over the number of products the display holds. You may be able to use your co-op advertising budget to cover the costs. However, the co-op allowance (5%) is controlled the by the retailer buyer and he or she would have to approve this cost.

Display vehicles are used for a number of reasons:

- Test new products
- New Product introductions
- Seasonal products
- Promotional products

Research your options online:

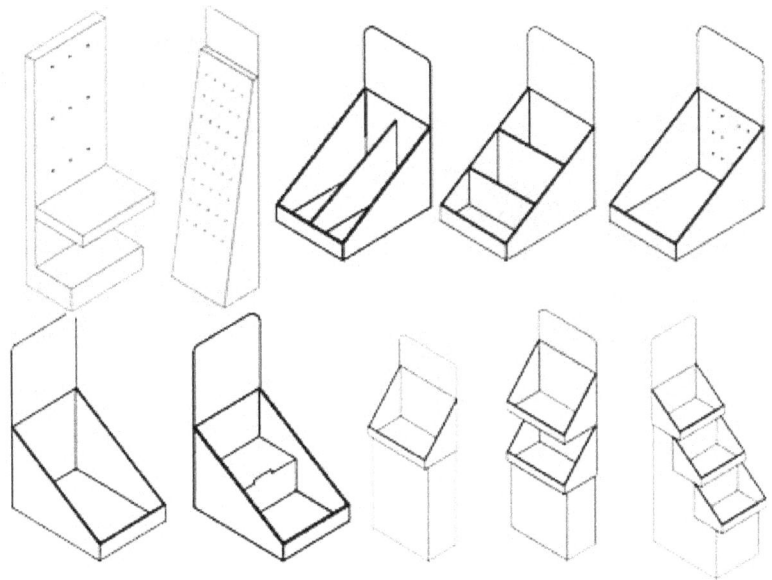

Side Kicks

Side-kicks are cardboard units that fit into a grid system and hang on the side of the end-caps. You can create a cardboard header to increase brand and product awareness. The product is shipped inside the side-kick and the store personnel simply take out the display unit from its outer shell, attach the header and it is stocked and ready to go.

This is an expensive way to feature your product. Not all major retailers use side-kicks - the ones that do, like them. You pay for the side-kick ($6-$10 each –or more) depending on size and if it is made domestically or in China. It only has a one-time use. Once the product is sold, the display is thrown out.

If your products are small, and you can merchandise a large quantity of products in a side-kick, then it may be an option as you will be amortizing the cost of the display over the number of products it contains. It is a great way to create instant brand and product awareness at store level.

Dimensions are approximately 58" high x 12" wide x 4" deep. To confirm the actual size, check with your rep or retailer.

Floor Stand

A cardboard floor display stands alone on the floor. You can take your side-kick unit and simply create a base for it and turn it into a floor stand. It only involves an extra cost for the cardboard base. Also an expensive investment, but worth it if you have an opportunity to test your product this way with a major retailer. Your product is much more visual out in the open surrounded by graphics than fighting for attention on the shelf down an isle. A floor stand also comes pre stocked.

Not all retailers use floor stands so, again, check with your rep.

Counter Display Unit

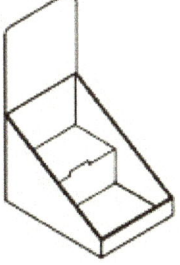

This is a cardboard display that sits on a shelf or a counter. It is already pre packed with product and when you open the box and rearrange the cardboard flaps, it turns into a display unit with a header attached. These display units are a wonderful way for your product to get noticed. Prepack units are usually promotional/seasonal displays and have a limited shelf life.

Clip Strips

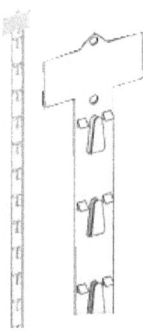

These are white or clear plastic strips approximately 2" wide x 24" long. The strips have twelve peg hooks attached to them. They, in turn, attach to the planogram areas down the isles. Although not all retailers use clip strips, they are another great vehicle for merchandising your carded product outside the shelf area. Retailers like to see an 85% sell through on their promotional products before they consider them for their planogram sections.

    It is not difficult to mock up these display units in your computer using the same graphics as your packaging. Make sure you have researched the costs and how much product fits in the units. You will need this information for your sales materials.

End Caps

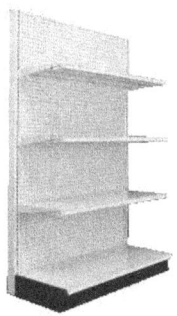

These are the shelf areas usually three feet or four feet wide at the end of the isles. Each category has a certain number of end caps they can use in the store. These end caps are prime retail space (like beachfront property). Sometimes there is a charge for featuring your item on an end cap, sometimes not. It all depends on the retailer and the buyer. Often more than on manufacturer share an end cap. The buyer may be using an end cap for a particular theme or to promote a hot item. These end caps are used promotionally. The life span of an end cap can range from thirty to sixty days. Often buyers prefer to use the end cap for items they carry in their planogram section so there is a home for the merchandise that didn't sell.

When Caboodles cosmetic cases were introduced during 1987-1988 there was no home for them at retail. Buyers chose to put the cases on end caps - which created instant brand recognition at store level. Our media support through Teen Magazines encouraged buyers to promote the products in store and through their roto (coupon) advertising.

Choosing Your Manufacturer

This is the time to decide if you want to manufacture your product yourself, or not.

If you choose to manufacture the product yourself you may have a choice of manufacturing the product domestically or overseas.

Manufacturing Domestically

The benefit of manufacturing the product domestically is the ability to service your customers in a more-timely manner. The disadvantage of manufacturing your product domestically is the potentially higher costs involved.

Higher manufacturing costs not only affect the end retail price of your product but leaves you vulnerable when overseas manufacturers decide to compete with you.

If your product is very large, and would therefore incur high freight costs, then manufacturing your product domestically may prove to be more cost effective in the long run.

If, during your research, you find your competitors' products are made domestically, then you need to research what manufacturers do custom manufacturing (making products for other companies not just their own branded products). Search an online search for "Manufacturers Association of America".

Manufacturing Overseas

Manufacturing your product overseas reduces the product cost (and packaging and display costs) but requires a longer lead-time to get the product to market.

- 30 days to order materials
- 30 days to make the product
- 30 days to ship to product to your USA port

You will also need to warehouse some inventory in the USA once your product is placed in retail planograms as retailers will require regular and fast shipments to their stores in order to re-stock their shelves.

The first step is to look at similar products in the marketplace and see where they are manufactured. If these products say "Made in China" then in order to reach the required retail price points, you may need to source your product in China also.

In the early 90s I began to source products in China. Hong Kong was still separate from China then. I would be taken into little villages inside China to meet with my factories. It was a very different country then. Factories were basic and the workers lacked marketing skills. They simply made a product to its specifications. Since then China has become the manufacturing capital of the world. I wish I was given a penny for every time I heard, "but the quality of China made products is inferior". This is not true. The Chinese are wonderful craftsmen. I used to stay in some of the most beautiful hotels in the world. Marble staircases, marble bathrooms, handcrafted wood ships made out of matchsticks adorned the huge lobbies. Factory owners began to send their children to be educated overseas. They returned with MBAs and product development, brand development and marking skills to match anyone in the USA corporate world. Wal-Mart, Target and other major retailers began to have products designed and developed in China. No longer did America have the marketing edge. Factory towns turned into bustling cities.

If you prefer to work directly with the factories you may want to visit the Canton Fair and meet with factories at the show and review the quality of their merchandise. You can hire a translator at the show who can communicate your needs directly with the different factories. I have attended these shows often and have been amazed at the wide range of products exhibited there.

THE CANTON FAIR CHINA IMPORT AND EXPORT FAIR

China Import and Export Fair, also known as the Canton Fair, is held biannually in Guangzhou every spring and autumn, with a history of 55 years since 1957.

The complex covers a total construction area of 1,100,000 M₂ with the indoor exhibition area of 338,000 M₂ and the outdoor exhibition area of 43,600 M₂. The Area A has an indoor exhibition area of 130,000 M₂ and an outdoor exhibition area of 30,000 M₂, the Area B has an indoor exhibition area of 128,000 M₂ and an outdoor exhibition area of 13,600 M₂, and the Area C has an indoor exhibition area of 80,000 M₂.

Address: No. 380, Yuejiang Zhong Road, Guangzhou, China

Chinese exhibitors of the Canton Fair boast good credibility and strength. Over 24,000 Chinese enterprises attend each session of the Fair. Among them, manufacturers account for 51%; foreign trade enterprises account for 38%; industrial trade enterprises account for 10% Has an exhibition area of 1.18 million square meters, the 116th session of the Canton Fair had over 60,000 exhibition stands, attracting 24,840 exhibitors from both home and abroad.

The Fair is a comprehensive one with the longest

history, the highest level, the largest scale, the most complete exhibit variety, the broadest distribution of overseas buyers and the greatest business turnover in China.

You need an invitation and a visa to attend which is easily arranged through their website.

For more information:
http://www.cantonfair.org.cn

Global Sourcing

You can also do global sourcing at **www.globalsourcing.com**. You may need to work through an agent (most agents work out of Hong Kong) or you can work with the factories direct. An agent can source all the materials and components required to manufacture your product along with the appropriate factories. He can obtain product cost estimates from your samples or mock-ups. He will also work with the factories through the product development process through to the manufacturing process. He will know what regions of China and the surrounding countries specialize in your particular type of product and can source the best factory or factories for you.

Once you have sourced a number of potential manufacturers, or have decided on a particular agent who specializes in manufacturing your type of product, you will need to go through the following steps.

Follow Up:

Earlier you researched manufacturers and supplies who specialized in your type of product. Have you added more suppliers to your original list based on further research? Who are they?

Have you sourced your product overseas, in particular through Canton Fair or global sourcing websites? What suppliers have you sourced?

Have you located an agent who can source your type of product overseas? Who?

Keep all your manufacturing and sourcing information carefully documented and filed.

Costing Your Product

In order to get a fairly accurate cost to manufacture your item, you will need a product sample or an accurate illustration of the product with dimensions, required materials, and projected quantities. Choose three different quantities for costing purposes. For example; twenty-five thousand units, fifty thousand units and one hundred thousand units of each item.
      This will give you an idea of what the volume discounts will be. If the factory thinks you are serious

about manufacturing the item in volume, they may make your product samples for free providing they do not require a mold, which could be cost prohibitive to them.

If your product requires a mold, get a cost for the initial mold and also the per-unit cost based on volume.

If you already have a major retailer's commitment to purchase your product, a Chinese manufacturer may be prepared to cover the cost of the initial mold or amortize the cost of the mold over a period of time.

Beware of choosing a factory that offers the lowest price or meets your cost requirements. Often a factory will agree to manufacture your product for a low price and then when you place a reorder to meet your retailers needs, they advise you that there is a price increase and now you have a problem making your desired margin as you have already presold the product to the retailer for an agreed upon price based on the original cost quotes.

To be safe it is often advisable to work with a couple of factories and obtain quotes and samples from both manufacturers so you have a back up if required.

Your manufacturer will ship your individual products in master cartons to your USA port and you will need to arrange freight to your USA warehouse/s. How many products you want to have in your master carton depends on the size of your product and the requirements of most major retailers. You need to ensure you have incorporated the price of handling and shipping your products in master cartons in your per unit cost.

Each individual product needs to be protected by cardboard dividers and wrapped in separate plastic bags inside the master carton. It is important that the products are not damaged during shipment. We would do a few test shipments first to ensure the products were well protected in shipment.

For Caboodles products we shipped four or six individual organizer boxes in one master carton. Obviously small products, such as lipsticks, would require many more products per master carton. Your manufacturer and your rep can advise you on this subject. You will need to know this information before you complete your price sheet.

As you are obtaining your price quotes from manufacturers or suppliers, know that you will be working on your final pricing once you have researched your whole pricing structure.

At this stage you are getting initial price quotes so that you are prepared for this exercise.

Can They do the Volume You Require?

It is important that the factory you choose can do the necessary volume required to supply your retailers.

Initially your product may be tested in various retail stores but once proven successful, you need to be prepared to supply large quantities within a ninety-day period. In order to do this your factory has to be able to source the fabric or materials and manufacture the product in the quantities you require.

Samples for your Reps And Buyers

As you begin to work with your chosen factory you will be developing product samples. This is a process that may require many attempts to get the product right. Sample products may be made out of a material that is immediately available to the factory and may not be exactly the material you prefer. However, make sure you have priced your product based on the preferred materials. If your sample products are fairly close to what your end product will look like, then you can use these samples for selling purposes.

If your product requires a mold before your product can be sampled, this is the time to have a prototype product made. This prototype model can be photographed and used in your sales book. The actual prototype can be used during your initial sell-in process. But as a new vendor, and you have yet to prove your credibility in the marketplace, most buyers will want to see an actual manufactured finished product before committing to buy. Your reps will be able to advise you in this area.

You will eventually need enough product samples for your first trade show and for your reps. The number of samples, obviously depends on how many products are in your line and how many you will need to create a visual "in store" presentation.

Photograph all your product samples and begin to create your product pages for your sales materials.

Follow Up:

How many product samples will you need for your initial sales presentations?

How many product samples will you need for your first trade show?

How many products will your Master Cartons hold?

Packaging Costs

Supply your factory with your packaging concepts. Provide an actual sample of the size of your packaging and the quality you prefer.

If you have a couple of different packaging ideas have both of them quoted. Keeping the cost down is crucial to your end product costs.

Warehousing Shipping And Distribution

Time for some online research. If you have chosen to go it alone and use a custom manufacturer to make your product and they do not provide the necessary warehousing, shipping and distribution services, then you will need to find a company who will handle this side of the business for you. If you are sourcing your product from China they will give you a product cost based on shipping your products to a USA shipping port.

This may all seem a bit daunting at first. But once you have done your research and talked to a number of companies specializing in this area you will feel a lot more comfortable with this aspect of the business. After all, you just want to get your product from the manufacturer into your retailers' warehouse. Once you are at this stage, you are sitting pretty.

Search the web for national warehousing and distribution services. There are established and reputable companies that specialize in all aspects of warehousing and distribution. Many companies have strategically located distribution centers throughout the county.

Research what states are best for your warehousing location or locations. The large retailers have multiple warehouse locations you will be required to ship to. Your warehouse location has an effect on your shipping costs.

Establish what company you will be using for your warehouse and shipping needs and obtain the necessary costs to incorporation into your product's selling price. If you selling price to the retailer does not include freight, then the retailers have agreed to incur this cost. However, you will still have to include your warehousing costs, your shipping costs from China or local manufacturer to your warehouse location, and the necessary handling and EDI costs that will be incurred with each order.

With products made in China during the initial testing period, we had a policy that we only brought in product to the US warehouse to cover orders and product samples. This prevents huge amounts of capital being tied up in inventory that is waiting to be sold.

This means that all orders you receive require a ninety-day lead time to get the product into your USA warehouse.

If you are fortunate enough to be planogrammed into a store's everyday shelf space then the retailer will require you to have back up stock to keep the shelves stocked at all times. This means that you will have to work with your rep and your buyer to create sales projections for the year so that you can warehouse enough product to cover the re-orders. Obviously this is a difficult task the first year as it is not easy to project how well your product will sell once it is on the shelf.

Carrying too much inventory in your warehouse can tie up a lot of your working capital. Keeping track of your inventory is crucial to your company's financial success.

Follow Up:

What custom warehouse and manufacturing companies can supply your needs?

Have you researched their EDI and bar code capabilities?

Have you itemized all the costs relating to getting your product from you manufacturer to the retailer's warehouse?

Pricing Your Product

If you are creating products in different sizes that require different price points now is the time to revisit a retail store. Look at your competition. If you don't have competition in your category then find products that are made out of similar materials and have a similar function.

For Helmet Toppers we were creating a new category. We had no other product to compare price pints with. However, we searched the stores and found a headband with plush animal ears attached and used this product as our price indicator. If we could offer our product slightly cheaper than the headband product our product would have a higher perceived value.

We also used the headband item as a price indicator to establish the prices for our whole product line. The Helmet Toppers product that was closest in size to the headband was priced accordingly (slightly cheaper) and all other products were priced based on relative size and perceived value.

If someone else is selling an item similar to yours for a certain retail price, then rest assured, you can do so too. If you are having problems getting the cost that you need there may be a number of reasons why this is happening.

- You may not be getting your costs from the right manufacturer. Find the country that specializes in making your type of item and get products from two or three factories.

- Your competitor may be doing a large volume in this particular item and therefore has negotiated a much lower cost.

- Your product design my be more complicated; see if you can simplify it to reduce cost. If not, ensure that your "added improvements" are clearly understood by the consumer.

As mentioned earlier, you wan to work out your selling price from the retail down. For example if the retailer is going to sell your product for $10 (retail price) and wants a 50% margin then you will be selling her the product for $5.

In order to do this you will need to know what margin the retailer expects to make on your item. Your rep can help you with this.

Every category in the store generates different margins. Every product type generates different margins.

What Costs are Involved?

Here is an outline of costs that will be incurred; you

will need to confirm these costs with your own sources but this will give you a general idea.

Co-op Advertising Allowance

Some retailers require a co-op advertising allowance. The retailers use this money to advertise your product direct to their customers. (advertising leaflets you receive online, in your Sunday papers or in the store)

These advertising ventures are profitable to the retailers and can be quite costly for the vendor (you). The standard rate is an agreed upon 5% of sales. Therefore, if you receive an order of $250,000 worth of merchandise then the most the retailer can deduct is $12,500 (5%)

It is based on a yearly accrual, which means that if the retailer does not use all of the accrued dollars before the end of the year, the balance goes back to zero.

It is also on a bill-back, proof of performance, basis - which means the retailer shows proof of using your product in their ad and sends you a copy of the ad along with the amount already deducted off your next invoice. (They are not supposed to deduct the money until you have received proof).

Note: sometimes you may choose to let the retailer use this 5% for in-store prime positioning such as end caps, promotional isles etc.

Coupons/Store Ads

The buyer may request extra money for an actual advertising opportunity. This can be a large sum of money depending on the size of the account. Some ads cost over $50,000 for very large chains. Some cost more, some cost less.

Retailer ads prove to be very successful because of the much larger sales volume generated during the life of the ad.

Also, if your product is chosen to be included in one of their ad's then usually the retailer needs to purchase much larger quantities for the ad period. The buyer has to achieve certain sales levels during the ad promotional period. Being chosen for an ad is a blessing and a curse. It can be cost prohibitive for a small sized company and yet, the opportunity for a large order and the increased brand and product awareness the ad generates is very tempting.

New Store Allowances

Retailers often ask for a 5% new store allowance. This 5% only relates to their new store opening order. This allowance assists them with setting up the planogram, stocking the new store, etc. Often there are only a handful of new stores a year per customer so this allowance is not a huge expense. But one to be aware of.

Additional Retailer Discounts

Every retailer has a different type of promotional or advertising expense that may require an extra 5% discount. It is a good idea to keep 5-10% out for emergencies.

For example if the buyer requests a floor stand, this cost has to be added to your product cost and yet you still have to keep the retails competitive. If you have not allowed for this extra cost in your price structure then this expense may eat away all your profit margin. Other unexpected discounts could include an end cap display allowance (end of isle price promotional space).

Freight Charges

Some retailers may want you to pay the freight to their US warehouses. This can add a considerable expense to your product. If you find that most of your customers insist on having the freight paid then this should be part of your cost analysis. We find that more and more larger customers accept FOB (freight on board) terms; smaller customers may require you to pay the freight, so do your research before you finalize your price sheet.

If you are shipping your product from China your factory can give you the freight costs involved in shipping the product to a port in the USA or Canada.

There are companies that will warehouse, distribute, and offer EDI (Electronic Data Exchange) facilities, etc. They will assist you with your internal freight costs and program.

Some retailers may want to purchase your product FOB (freight on board) China or Hong Kong. This means the retailer will pay the freight from a shipping port in China or Hong Kong.

They are already bringing over container loads of product and it may be more cost effective for them to add your product to one of their containers. Of course they will expect you to discount the cost of the product to reflect your reduced freight cost.

Most overseas customers prefer to purchase product FOB China or FOB Hong Kong. You will need to give them pricing based on this scenario. For these overseas customers (either retailers or distributors) who are purchasing from you in large container loads you can give them a price that may only be 25% above your cost as you will not be incurring all the costs incurred in marketing and selling your product plus all their retailer discounts, co-ops and rep commissions. They need to be able to offer your products at a competitive price.

Most USA companies prefer to purchase from your USA warehouse. Then it is simply a matter of establishing whether or not their program includes freight to their warehouse locations or not.

You will have to price your freight costs from China to your USA warehouse location and include these costs in your product price analysis.

I know all this information is a little overwhelming at first (I knew nothing about freight costs, shipping, and warehousing when I first started), but don't worry. Your reps will be advising you as to what their retailers expect when it comes to discounts, freight costs and advertising costs. This information is just a good reference point so you are not completely in the dark when these issues are discussed. The terminologies are also necessary if you need to do any online research or need to know what questions to ask your potential warehouse and shipping agents

Pricing from the Top Down

I create every product from the retail price point down. In other words, I create the product knowing what the retail has to be then I work from this price down to the cost price. Never make the mistake of creating a product from the cost up. When you are creating products for the mass retail market, price is as important as the product. If your product cannot be made for the cost required to achieve your desired retail you don't have a product yet. You will have to go back to the drawing board (so to speak) and start again.

Working Out Your Profitability

What is your desired retail? What margin will the store

take (50%)? This will be your selling price:

Per Unit Costs:
- Brand advertising – 3% - 5%
- Co-op Advertising 5%
- Bad Debts (e.g. 2%)
- Rep Commissions (e.g.7%)
- Freight costs to USA
- Freight Costs to Retailer
- Packaging Costs
- Retailer's Ad cost (if any)
- Display Costs (Floor Stand/side kick)
- Manufactured final cost per unit
- Amortized mold cost

Yes, you have to take all these costs into consideration before you can calculate your true selling price to the retailer.

Once you have established your desired retail price, selling price and your final product cost you can determine what your profit is and if it will work – Does it?

Your Product Costs are No Secret

Often the retailer is your biggest competitor. Most large retailers are already creating and manufacturing product in China. Retailers are bringing into their stores container loads of products from China they have created. Often these products are purchased specifically for a promotional period (a one time buy).

They know how much most products costs to manufacture. This doesn't mean to say that your retailer will simply knock you off but it does mean that they are usually aware of how much your product costs to manufacture.

A buyer from a major mass market retailer said to me during one of my presentations of a new innovative line of products, "I really like what you have. I will either buy them from you or copy them." I still remember that feeling of complete shock. Can he say that? I thought. This was my beautiful new innovative line of teen bath and body products. They looked so beautiful sitting on his office desk - all glittering in colored gels in funky shaped bottles. The same buyer brought his "guy" into our booth and showed him the same product line I had kept hidden behind curtains at the back of the booth.

That is why creating a brand is so important to your company's success. Retailers carry branded items because consumers buy branded items.

Retailers' products are private label (their own label). A major mass merchandiser, for example, has their own private label for helmets. They do not carry brand name helmets. This makes it almost impossible for us to sell them our Helmet Toppers accessories. Our only chance is to develop the brand and create consumer demand for our brand in order for them to consider purchasing our product.

It is, however, unlikely a retailer, or another manufacturer would compete with a new category or product line. They will wait until the category "has proven itself in the marketplace" before taking that risk. By then, you hope your brand has established itself in the category and is strong enough to survive any competition.

Once Caboodles had proven to be a viable category at retail competitors entered the marketplace. But by this time, Caboodles had proven itself to be the product and category leader (I made sure of that).

In fact, I became the first major competitor to Caboodles when I started my own company, Sassaby and could advance from employee to president.

Competing with my own "baby" and "first love" was difficult. In order to enter the teen girl market who were completely "Caboodlized" (some girls owning up to ten Caboodles each), it required a miracle.

I was so lucky that my many years of working in high school classrooms gave me an edge in the marketplace. I had become a teen trend expert and with the help of our teen focus groups I learned about a new television show that was fast becoming a teen favorite that year in the early 90s - Beverly Hills 90210. We preceded Nike and other major companies who later became licensees too. Our focus groups gave us the edge. The very first year we sold in $30 million at retail ($15 million at wholesale). We created a national promotion spearheaded by Shannon Doherty advising teen girls they could win a day on the set of Beverly Hills 90210 and meet the cast. Tori Spelling attended our Press Event in Los Angeles. It was exciting. Our Sassaby cosmetics organizers sat proudly on the retail shelves next to Caboodles organizers.

It wasn't until Sassaby was sold to Estee Lauder that the owner and manufacturer of Caboodles asked my new company to revitalize the Caboodles brand - which I was excited to do. As a consultant I could earn a percentage of sales and still be involved in my "first love". When we introduced Caboodles "Jellies" to the marketplace the manufacturer created the very first clear glitter plastic molded case in the industry. This new introduction (utilizing the same molds) instantly rejuvenated the product line and put excitement back into the category at retail. Buyers said "Caboodles is Back!"

We found our "Jellies" look in the classroom. Toni and I noticed during our focus groups that the teen girls were wearing clear colored glitter sandals and shoes. We purchased some of the sandals and took them back to the manufacturer and said, "if you can make Caboodles boxes in this "look" we will have a winner." We called the look "Jellies" Full-page ads in TEEN, Seventeen and other magazines promoted the new "Jellies" collection. (You can view this box on the front cover of this book.)

Sales Materials And Sales Calls

Your Price Sheet

Once you have confirmed all the costs involved in manufacturing, packaging, shipping, distributing, and selling your products you can create your price sheet,

Always keep your price sheets separate from your sales catalog as they may change faster than your product information. Date each price sheet so you can keep track of what price sheet you have sent to a rep or buyer. You don't want to be changing your prices on a regular basis. There has to be a good reason for a price increase i.e. new innovative material etc.

You may need three separate price sheet:
- Retail Price Sheet – Domestic
- Distributor Price Sheet – Domestic
- International Distributor Price Sheet

Each price sheet should have the following information:

- Item Number
- Product Name
- Product Description
- UPC number
- Product Dimensions

- Case Size – (How many products in a master carton)
- Product Price

You can also add suggested retail if you feel it appropriate. But, check with your reps as most major retailers like to set their own retails as each retailer works off a slightly different margin.

The Sales Book

Twenty years ago I created all my product pages in PowerPoint and printed out glossy color copies and kept them in a binder. I like to have hard copies of what I am selling. Also I find during the creative process – my product pages change as I collect more and more data, focus group information, industry stats, trends etc.

    I called my book "The Sales Book". It is your first working sales manual. Until your product line is completely finalized you will be using this book as your sales manual. This information will be used for raising capital (if needed) , hiring reps, working with your graphic artists, working with product designers, engineers, printers and manufacturers.

    As time progresses and you are ready to go on your road show to sell to buyers, your "Sales Book" will be condensed into a product catalog. Your PowerPoint "sales book" presentation may also be requested by buyers -so keep it current.

Always use glossy paper for all your color images.

Front Cover

The front cover (which I update constantly) features your new logo, you one sentence and a photo of your product model or prototype.

For example: Our Helmet Toppers front cover featured our logo "Critter Gear for Helmet Wear" and a photo of our dog ears and nose on a helmet. Simple, colorful, fun and effective.

Page 1 – What is "Your Product?"

First Paragraph – Describe your Brand – what does it stand for?
Second Paragraph – What are your products?
Third Paragraph – Who is your target market?

Page 2 – The Industry

Now is the time to use all the research you did on the industry. The size of the market, the trends in the industry, etc.

You could be selling to a buyer who is new to the category and this information will be interesting to him. If it is a buyer who has been in the industry for years he will know you have done your homework. It is important to use stats that show the potential volume your product could degenerate. Remember, you need to be an expert on your product and how it relates to its industry.

Page 3 – The Category

- The size of the category – dollar volume, any trends etc.
- Recent growth of the category or a related trend in the category

You are looking for information that gives credibility to your product idea.

Pages 4-6 Focus Group Information

- Photos of consumers using your product with captions
- Information you have obtained and tallied from your numerous focus groups

Never, never, change your stats to suit your purpose. Your reputation in the marketplace is hard earned. Your credibility, integrity, and honesty is your protection in the business world, not a weakness.

In order to gain your rep's and buyer's respect you must always be honest. If you don't know an answer don't make one up. Just say "Let me get back to you on that". Better to give accurate information than wrong information; it will come back to haunt you.

Pages 7-12 - Your Products

In my sales book I like to feature two products per page. Obviously it makes sense to feature the items as they relate to each other. "A picture says a thousand words." Make sure your product pictures are of the highest quality and printed on glossy paper.

If your product looks better in use, then use these pages to show your product with the packaging. Use photos that show your product in the best way possible. Don't forget that every item has a model number and a UPC number.

Pages 13-14 – Packaging

If your product looks best photographed in its packaging then this is how you should feature it. It is important to show a selection of products with the packaging so that the retailer can see what he is actually buying for his stores.

Pages 15-17 – Merchandising Vehicles

Feature photos or illustrations of your promotional display units along with the dimensions, number of products, item number and UPC number.

Marketing Your Product

A good rule of thumb is to budget 3% - 5% of sales for consumer and trade advertising. This fund can also be used for your PR budget.

If you project you will be selling one million dollars at wholesale then you would have thirty to fifty thousand dollars in your consumer advertising budget.

Don't get this confused with our co-op advertising. This is a separate fund that you, the owner of the brand, commit to spend.

Once your sales reach the ten million dollar mark then your budge is a lot healthier at three hundred to five hundred thousand dollars.

When you sales reach the one hundred million dollar mark then your budget is three to five million dollars. Then you can really have some fun.!

Of course the super size companies have marketing budgets over sixty million dollars. I have never played in that field. However my daughter does.

Where to advertise depends on your type of product, who your consumer is, what volume you want to generate, what your initial financial investment commitment is, and whether you are planning on selling your products to brick and mortar retailers, online retailers or both. Just remember, you cannot compete with your retail customers. Caboodles products are sold today in both mass market retailers such as Wal-Mart, Target and also on Amazon.com. (over a dozen different styles on Amazon.com)

Twenty-five years ago we only had teen magazines to promote our teen products. Today with social media marketing has taken on a new face. As I am now a writer and indie publisher, I use social media on a daily basis for marketing and promoting my books.

Consumer Advertising

Print Advertising

Boy, how things have changed since I created Caboodles and Sassaby and product lines of toys and games and baby gear. Print was the place to be seen. It was so easy. TEEN magazine was a major player in the development of the Caboodles Brand. Every issue we filled with Caboodles boxes in hot teen colors. Advertorials (combination ad and editorial) were six pages long. Girls carrying Caboodles boxes, using Caboodles boxes - you get the general idea. We also advertised in Seventeen Magazine, Glamour Magazine and Mademoiselle Magazine.

Today there is still Teen Vogue, Seventeen Magazine, American Cheerleader, Twist, Girl's life etc.

Magazine advertising is expensive and today it is only one small piece of the consumer marketing pie. Now there are so many options to choose from.

Ad agencies lived off our marketing dollars. They created our ads and purchased the advertising space - they made a killing. Today companies such as fiverr.com offers creative services for mere dollars and you can always purchase advertising space at the last minute and save over 50% of their usual advertising costs. Do your research. Check out the consumer magazines that your consumers are reading and call them and ask for rate cards.

Once you have created your ad, have a copy included in your sales materials along with your proposed advertising plan.

Check with your advertising departments of your consumer magazines to enquire if they offer any new customer rates or promotional opportunities. Although the advertising department and the editorial department are completely separate, you may be able to generate a relationship with the magazine like we did over the years. Sometimes you can buy space at the last minute for a cheaper rate. Check it out.

I was invited to TEEN magazine's corporate offices in New York during the Caboodles years to talk to their advertising staff. They booked me a room at the Waldorf Astoria Hotel and I spent the following morning talking to their advertising staff about my loyal commitment to the magazine over the years. I loved working with TEEN and their personnel. It was a win-win for both of us. They had a supportive advertiser in us and we had a leading teen magazine who gave us instant credibility with our teen consumer.

There is not doubt that TEEN was an instigator in making Caboodles the biggest teen girl brand in the early 90s.

So partnering up with a consumer magazine is certainly advantageous to a brand's success.

As the Caboodles volume increased, so did our consumer ad spending. We used Hollywood photographers and top models. Our ad agency was wonderful. Nothing is more exciting than watching "your baby" become successful. I loved every minute of it. My job was to manage every ad shoot, every TEEN shoot advertorial shoot, and every PR event.

When to Advertise?

As "back to school" and "holiday" were our two main promotional seasons, most of our consumer advertising dollars were spent during these times.

Generally products will sell the most volume during holiday periods – Thanksgiving through the day after Christmas (which we call Boxing Day in New Zealand). The "five day stretch from Thanksgiving kicks off the digital holiday shopping season.

The Adobe data shows, in 2016, shoppers spent $3.35 billion on Black Friday and $3.45 billion on Cyber

Monday (an increase of 12.1%) And, at that time were predicting November and December sales to rise 3.6 percent to $655.8 billion. The major bricks-and-mortar chains grew their online sales 2 1/2 times the rate of smaller retailers. "They've figured out the key, which we're are seeing is really combination of social and mobile and email: says Adobe's vice president of marketing and customer insights.

Data from the National Retail Federation Consumer survey found that 3 million fewer people visited stores over Black Friday weekend, while 5.5 million more shopped online. As the move from store to digital continues to grow, it has one major advantage for product developers and marketers. We now have affordable choices when it comes to advertising to our consumers. When we were limited to print and television and advertising agencies held the strings, it was easy to target market our consumer.

I remember the day when there was no "fast forwarding TV ads" your consumers were a sitting audience. Today, recorded by Marketing Charts Study, traditional TV viewing is declining especially with the 18–34 year old viewer. (Streaming is at least partly to blame for Millennials' decisions to forego pay-TV.) However older consumers are still TV watchers with 21.2% of weekly adult viewers of broadcast TV are aged 65 plus. An interesting statistic (2016), among online adults, those in the 18-24 bracket are 52% more likely than average to watch TV programs online in a typical months.

Now cyber marketing has opened the gates to consumer marketing and, along with it, comes a surge of social media choices – Facebook, Twitter, YouTube, your website and so, so, many more.

Your products may have an additional peak season (e.g. Father's Day)– refer to your industry research materials.

So when to spend your consumer marketing budget is obviously when shoppers are shopping – online and in-store. Research your own product category and budget your ad dollars accordingly.

Web Marketing

Of course your website is one of your most important consumer brand awareness vehicles and doubles as your online pitch to your retail customers. When we launched Caboodles in 1987, the web was in its infancy. Now, at a swipe of a finger, or a click of a mouse, both your retail customers and your consumers can view your complete product line, be exposed to your brand, order online, and become involved in your marketing strategies. Involving your consumer with your brand is the way of the future. No longer is there a middle – man - your brand is exposed to the world and you have complete control.

Now that I am a writer and publisher, I can take my product (book) from the mind to the marketplace in just a few weeks (depending on the size of the book) and have it available online worldwide. What an incredible marketing age we are living in.

Setting up your website is easier than ever. I have being using GoDaddy as my web manager and Wordpress as my website vehicle – which is easy to use. I have all my header graphics designed by www.fiverr.com. I purchase images from online photography websites and keep my website up to date. The same applies to my other social media sites such as Facebook, YouTube, Linkedin and Twitter. Daily posts and updates keep my social media sites relevant. Get a quick product trailer created using an online graphic designer from Fiverr (so professional but so affordable) and play it on YouTube.

Your tweets and posts should be informative not just promotional! Entice your customers with a tease to visit your website.

Your website is your worldwide catalog. Show your products in the best light. Keep loyal to your brand. Keep loyal to your consumer. Don't try to be everything to everyone or will end up "messing up your brand". Became a social media marketing expert.

Trade Advertising

You have done your trade advertising research and know the relevant trade magazines and websites you need to participate in.

When your product is on the shelves you hope that your PR agency has managed to get you great editorial coverage in these magazines. Time to advertise is when you have become a little more established. If however, you have been successful in a major product launch, then a paid advertisement in a relevant category or product article would be appropriate and a very effective way to create brand awareness with your retail customers.

Remember to follow all your retailers on Twitter and Facebook. Hopefully some will follow you in return. Keep your daily posts relevant to the industry – post the latest statistics in your industry, keep a blog on your website informing your customers of new trends, what your product category is doing worldwide, and any consumer research that is relevant to your particular industry.

Consumer Shows

A consumer show is an industry show that is for the general public (not retailers). Examples of consumer shows are: The Home Show, Surf and Dive shows, travel shows, Cheerleading shows, etc. Manufacturers and suppliers can exhibit their products in individual booths. We would exhibit our Caboodles products at the major cheerleading camps. Check out your consumer shows that relate to your product category and find out what opportunities there are for you to show your product. It is a great way to get product and brand awareness for little cost and great feedback.

Consumer Competitions/Events

Caboodles was a sponsor the "Miss Teen" competition for many years. We gave away product to all the contestants and a grand prize to the winner. Our products were featured during the television show and we ran our TV advertisement during the event. Amazing coverage. Great brand builder. I was also a judge for Miss Teen USA on year it was a fun experience.

It reminded me when I had to organize the annual "Miss New Zealand" competition in the mid 1980s before I came to America. As the owner of a local model agency (and a television personality at the time) I was asked to organize the event. I arranged the show venue at one of our large shopping malls in the middle of Christchurch city.

The contestants walked out onto a large carpeted ramp, which had been erected on the ground floor of the mall. I had organized with the local police to secure the area as we expected very large crowds. The mall was packed with onlookers. Shoppers were hanging over the balconies watching the event. All of a sudden a group of female protestors began to throw live mice over the balconies and onto the ramp. Models scattered, people creamed, Police came running, and the competition suddenly became the biggest news event of the year. I remember my phone never stopped ringing. Reporters wanted interviews – it was a nightmare. I had a violent headache for weeks.

    I had a much better success when we ran a national USA "Miss Caboodles" competition. We held the final event on the beach at Santa Monica, California. The winner would win a makeover and appear in TEEN magazine. The whole group stayed at the recently built Loews Hotel on the waterfront. My suite had a white grand piano and amazing views of the ocean – quite a change from my simple life back in New Zealand.

What magazine have you chosen as your first choice?

What consumer events could you attend or donate products to?

What consumer shows could you display product at?

Getting the Word Out

    Public Relations (PR) is the most cost effective way of gaining brand and product awareness. Whether it is simply giving away free product to your consumers or getting your product featured on a television morning talk show, it is extremely powerful.

PR versus conventional advertising is perceived as more credible by the consumer. A magazine editor writing about your product is far more believable than an advertisement featuring your product.

We gave away thousands of Helmet Toppers to participants of skateboarding competitions and bicycle rides nationwide. We always provided on-the-set movie studios with Caboodles hoping they would feature them in their teen bedroom sets (which they often did). Just recently I saw one of our Caboodles boxes being used on the Project Runway TV Series. Creating brand and product awareness is essential to a successful retail launch. The more familiar your consumer is with your product before she walks down the retail isle the more impact your product will have on her. However, you don't want to be advertising your product before the consumer can find it online or in-store.

Most of the national magazines are spearheaded out of the New York area where your PR agency should be located. Your agency can be hired on a per assignment basis or on a monthly retainer. I prefer a monthly retainer as PR work is a constant requirement during the life of a brand.

Your first task is to create your press release which will be used at your first trade show and will be distributed to all trade and consumer magazines when your product is due to launch into the marketplace.

You will have two versions of your press release. One for trade magazines and one for consumer magazines.

Your PR agency will write and distribute your press releases along with product photos and product samples. If you are a competent writer, you may want to create your own PR materials and place them in the Press Room prior to the show. You can check with the show organizers the appropriate schedule and obtain a list of press attendees so you can follow up after the show. You can also research the list of editors specializing in your product category and email a short press release prior to the show inviting them to your booth.

Daily newspapers, television news programs and community clubs and associations are also part of your PR blitz.

If you are hiring a PR agency get them involved in the early stages so they are fully versed with all the necessary industry and product information necessary to develop their PR strategies and programs.

Time to Do Your Check List

Before your product or product line goes on the road show it is time to do your final check list:

- Do you have your business structure in place?
- Are your retail price points acceptable to the industry now that you have finalized your costs?
- Is your packaging acceptable to the industry and the consumer?
- Does your packaging tell the story?
- Is your sales book complete?
- Do you have your price sheets finalized?
- Have you confirmed your program (i.e. coop allowances, retailers' discounts, shipping costs etc.?
- Do you have your mock up display units?
- Do you have your story rehearsed?
- Do you have your one sentence description of your product perfected?
- Do you have your brand identity and logo finalized?
- Are your products in a saleable form (i.e. sample, prototype,)?
- Have you done all your research? Can you talk intelligently about your product's category and industry?
- Are you armed with all your focus group statistics confirming your product's credibility?

- Do you know who your consumer is?
- Have you set up your national rep force?
- Do you have the right attire for your sales presentations? Have you checked out the dress code expected by your customers? (Yes, different retailers have different dress codes)

You may only have ten minutes allotted to your presentation. I have found that times vary depending on the customer. Sometimes I am allotted one hour for a new product presentation, but often times only ten to twenty minutes is all you have. First impressions are important. After all the hard work you have done don't forget to look as good as your product. You are your product. Your story is your product's story.

Do you have your presentation down? Have you practiced it over and over again? Is it clean, clear, precise, interesting, exciting, informative, and humble? (You will be leaving your ego at home).

Practice your presentation on a family member or a friend. You don't want to stumble and stammer your way through your presentation. Practice makes perfect. No product ends up on a retail shelf without someone selling it.

If you feel you have all the ammunition you need to sell your product but do not feel that you can communicate it to the buyer, have your rep do the presentation for you. If you choose this route, your rep has to be your voice and you will need to schedule time with him to educate him on all aspects of your product.

You are the visionary and the inventor of the product and give your product its credibility so it is obviously better for you to do the presentation if you can.

Going On Your Road Show

Preparation is the key to success. When you have samples or prototypes of your products, have your sales book put together and sent sales packages out to your reps. Now you are ready to make your first sales call.

A finished product is like a car without fuel. It may look great, all the parts are there, but it is not going to go anywhere without energy.

Making my first sales call to a new retail account feels like auditioning for the X Factor. You have about two minutes to establish credibility and hope that you will be good enough to get a call back. I have been in a number of meetings that have generated five million dollar verbal orders within the first thirty minutes. I have also been in meetings when my products and I have been so strongly rejected that I simply cried myself to sleep that night.

As your products begin to prove themselves at store level and buyers start to get excited by the increase in their department's sales, you begin to enjoy your twice-yearly meetings with your major buyers.

In the late 1980s when Caboodles had become a number one teen brand, we used to have such fun meetings with the major retailers. One of my favorite mass retailers (and one of my favorite buyers at the time) used to come to our hotel for our new product presentation meetings. We, my rep and I, would set up a large conference room with new product prototypes, media ads, trend boards, story boards, and focus group analysis on six foot tables and for over an hour I would present the latest teen trends and product trends for the coming year. In those days, before the cyber world took over, new products were a main focus.

I usually tried to come in the night before a major meeting. Especially if it was winter and the meeting was on the east coast. The risk that my flight may be cancelled and I would not be able to make the meeting would not be an option.

I liked to allow extra time to visit a store with my rep prior to the meeting. Especially if this retailer did not have stores in California where my office was located. It is important to be familiar with their store layout, promotional opportunities, category merchandise, etc. so you can talk intelligently with the buyer regarding your product opportunities.

Your Check List

Be prepared. Preparation means covering all the bases. Here is a check list you must go through before every sales call:

- A separate sales package for all attendees.
- Background information relating to the retail customer: i.e.

Number of Stores?
What promotional vehicles they use in their stores (floor stands etc.)?
When do they set their planogram? How often?
Is the retailer financially sound? (You don't want to ship them $5 million worth of product and have them go into receivership the next month – yes it happens.

Do some research on the buyer. How long has he or she been buying this category? Will he or she be able to relate to your product (Does he or she have children the age of your consumer, etc.)? Is he or she the decision maker or have to get approval to purchase your product for upper management?

If, at all possible, have your rep set up ahead of time a conference room for the meeting, especially if you have a lot of visual collateral, products and merchandising display units to present. This takes the buyer out of his office and puts him in a neutral environment. It also enables you to control the setting. Allow a good ten minutes to set up.

If you have to present in a buyer's office, you will be limited to the size of his office and the space has available - usually the corner of his desk and the floor area.

I have made presentations jammed between isles in a retailer's stock room balancing my product samples on empty boxes and my knees. You do what you have to do.

Check how many people will be present at the meeting to ensure you have enough sales materials to distribute.

Prepare your product samples/prototypes etc. and any display vehicles you have mocked up. Wrap them in bubble wrap for protection. (Make sure you only have the display vehicles that this particular retailer can use in his stores.) Ensure you have quick and easy access to the merchandise so you can set up quickly once you are in the buyer's office or conference room. If time is limited you may need your rep to display the product in the room while you begin to make the presentation.

The Presentation

I have been making sales presentations for all of my working years. Practice makes perfect. It takes many presentations until they run smoothly. Don't worry, just relax, be yourself and enjoy it.

There are certain rules that I have learned along the way.

Never sit next to the buyer or too close to the buyer. Everyone has a certain space that they subconsciously keep protected. You never want to enter that space until you feel you can. Position yourself across the table and to one side of the buyer. You rep can sit next to the buyer or directly across from the buyer as he already has a relationship with the buyer and works alongside the buyer during the business process.

If you are setting up a room prior to the meeting, place all your sales materials in the position around the table where you want the buyer or buyers to sit. If you are making a presentation in the buyer's office and your chair is too close to his desk. You can move the chair back and position your briefcase etc. in front of your chair so you can provide the preferred space between you and the buyer. No one likes a sales person in his or her face.

Look at what angle the buyer has his books and papers on the desk. If they are placed straight, not on an angle, then make sure your materials are also positioned straight on the table. If you make the presentation with all the visuals off kilter it may cause an unconscious irritation to the buyer.

After initial introductions, always let your rep introduce you, your background (briefly) and the purpose why you are there. You do not want to be the first one to do the talking.

You want to present yourself as the inventor of the product idea and the owner, not a salesperson. Your rep is your salesperson. (Even though at the meeting you will be doing most of the talking - and the selling). However, there are exceptions to this rule. If you know you will have trouble communicating with the buyer (i.e. you don't speak his language) then the rep will make the presentation on your behalf after he has introduced you.

Never ask a question you want an affirmative answer to before you know the answer is going to be "yes". This is very important. Once you get a "no" it will be almost impossible to reverse the decision.

Offering a choice to get a positive answer is often the best way to initiate a commitment by the buyer. (i.e. Which size do you prefer – the $29.99 retail or the $9.99 retail?) That is one reason why you have multiple products to choose from.

When you feel the time is right (you are getting a positive response) involve the buyer in your presentation. (Pass him a product to look at or a document). Do not involve him physically in any portion of the presentation until you feel he is willing to participate. If you do this too early in the presentation and he is not receptive, he can subconsciously begin to reject the product.

You are your product. Your story is the product's story. Your credibility is your product's credibility.

Always show the utmost respect for the buyer's opinion and your rep's opinion. They are the experts in their field. Listen and learn. Any suggestions they make concerning improvements to the product or the packaging is worth researching with your consumer. And in many cases worth incorporating into your finished product or your next product.

Always sell your products from the lowest price point to the highest price point.

Never forget to ask for the order. Of course, the buyer cannot write an order there and then, there is a process from "I am definitely interested in buying this product" to an actual order. You must however establish the buyer's interest and confirm his interest verbally, in detail (and write down the details) before the meeting is adjourned.

Follow Up After the Meeting

Type out a call report. This report is for your internal use only. It should detail the meeting information; date, place, time, who attended the meeting, buyer profile, rep profile, presentation details, what products were shown, buyer response to each product, promotional opportunities, everyday planogram opportunities, outcome, etc. Do not expect your rep to do this. This is critical information for your next meeting and should be filed away for future reference.

Send a follow up email to the buyer thanking him for his time and outlining the meeting's major discussion points. Some reps prefer to do the follow up contact. Check with your rep if he is taking on this responsibility or if he wants you to do it.

Sent product samples and information as requested.

Getting the Order

There is usually quite a process that you need to go through before you receive that actual written order.

You will, however, get a verbal commitment to buy before you are expected to manufacturer and distribute the product. You usually don't receive the actual written order until approximately thirty days before you have to ship the product from your US warehouse.

This means it is difficult to obtain finance to manufacture the product based on an order. Especially if you are manufacturing the product in China and the lead-time is ninety days. Your rep can advise you more accurately when you can expect an order based on the particular retail customer but don't expect to get a written order ninety days prior to ship – this ins not usual procedure.

From Buyer Interest To Written Order

The process from your buyer showing an interest in ordering your product to an actual written order can take from a few short weeks to months.

During the meeting, if the buyer says he would like to test the product first. As, how many stores? What season would the products be tested in? How many items is he looking at testing? Does he require signage or a display? What would the ship date be? How long would the test run? Does he require a set of samples to present internally?

If the test is successful, would he consider your product for the planogram? What percentage sell through does he require to planogram the product as an every day item? (85%?)

Your rep usually takes notes during the meeting and your responsibility is to write a detailed report following every sales meeting. (The Call Report) This enables you to accurately follow up with an email to the buyer, within the next day or two, thanking him for his time, confirming the outcome of the meeting and detailing the product item numbers he is interested in buying. (and remember to copy the rep).

Your rep's responsibility is to follow up with the buyer to reconfirm his interest and to enquire if the test is a go ahead (the buyer may need to get approval to do the test from his upper management).

Paperwork has to be executed before an order can be written. You may have to provide proof of insurance documentation (research this online). The retailer will provide you with a vendor number.

First you will receive a verbal order giving quantity commitment and ship date. Then finally, the order is written.

Then it is time to celebrate. Don't forget to enjoy the successes. They are hard earned and are result of your tenacity and your creativity. Congratulate yourself!

Your Sales Pitch

Establish your credibility. Begin the presentation with your story, your background as it relates to the product idea, why or how you came up with the idea etc.

Briefly describe your product(s) and what you will be presenting to him.

Establish credibility for the product, industry, category, focus group stats. (You may want to have a visual of these stats).

Return back to the products and review them in more detail. Begin to ask questions (once you feel you will get a positive response). Your first questions should be "What do you think of the product? Do you think it is an item for your stores?"'

Listen to the buyer's response. Take notes as he is talking to you.

I learned something very important which has helped me with my presentations over the years. I always wanted everyone to like me. I wanted everyone to like my products. And I knew that these two desires were closely linked. I was my product and if a buyer too an instant dislike to me I was shattered. I had one buyer who started throwing papers around her desk with such fury I though she was going to attack me.

What I learned was this; 20% of people love you for who you are – your personality, your energy, your quirks, etc. 20% of people dislike you for exactly the same traits, and 60% of people don't really care either way.

This took so much pressure off my shoulders. I realized that you cannot make everyone like you. If you find a buyer takes an instant dislike to you, have your rep make the presentation and make yourself as unnoticeable as possible.

Do You Have A Viable Product?

Time to stop, regroup, and ask yourself the important question; Do I have a feasible product that can be manufactured, marketed, and sold at a desirable price?

You do not want to continue until you are sure you have a product that will sell. This means you have to run enough focus groups to confirm the product's viability with your consumer and you have received positive feedback, from your reps and at least a couple of retailers.

Now is the time to pull the plug if your product idea has not been received well by the marketplace. I loved the book *Who Moved My Cheese* by Spencer Johnson and Kenneth Blanchard. If you have not read it. do so. It talks about facing change and how we handle it. It also talks about denial which is one of the traits that product developers seem to have. You can't afford to be in denial if you just don't have a viable product.

If however, you have done your homework and your product idea has been approved by both your consumer and your potential buyers, then it is time to proceed to the next stage of development. This is where you will begin to spend money and you may need to raise some capital in order to begin your manufacturing process.

You can now use all the information you have been gathering to create a strong business plan which will be required to raise the desired capital.

Once you are at the final stages of your product development and have nailed down your manufacturing costs it is a good time to begin working with a good CFO to button up all your costs and work on your financial projections. Make sure you always have access to good financial advice and good legal advice. Staff up as required.

Manufacturing Your First Run

If your product requires a mold to be made now you will be approving the final mold design and going to the next stage of having your mold made. This requires another capital investment. The smaller the mold the less expensive the product – you should have already confirmed and approved your mold costs and designs.

If your retailers would not commit to a verbal order without seeing the finished product, you have to make a decision based on the reception you have received from both the consumer and the retailers. It is your call to decide to go ahead with making the mold and having initial products made before receiving a verbal commitment to buy.

If our product does not require a mold then you are ready to proceed with your fist "run" of products. If your products are being manufactured in China, remember it takes 30 days to order the fabric, 30 days to manufacture the products and 30 days to ship the product to your port of call.

Purchasing your Materials

Depending on the type of product you are making, you may have to purchase the first run of required materials in order to begin the manufacturing process. Make sure you have approved these materials and have received actual samples of the materials you are ordering. If samples are not available, then make sure you have given them a sample of the desired material you wish to purchase. Confirm costs based on initial quantities.

You should already have your US warehouse set up ready to receive and ship the product. And have set up your UPC Codes (bar codes) and EDI (electronic data interchange) requirements.

Estimating Initial Quantities

Be careful! Don't let your enthusiasm run away with you. Manufacturing costs money. Shipping products costs money. Product sitting in a warehouse costs money. Only product that is pre-sold is worth this capital investment.

Pre selling means that you have already called on retailers and they have made a verbal commitment to purchase your product and have given you actual quantities. Remember that a verbal commitment is a verbal commitment – not a written order. However, a written order is usually not given to you until thirty days before they expect the product to arrive in their warehouse. And it takes you ninety days to make and ship the product from China, a verbal commitment is usually all you will get before you begin your manufacturing process.

Be realistic! It is not a race. Now is the time to be strategic. Plan your first quantities based on your initial test orders. Remember to order enough finished product to supply your sales needs: i.e. rep samples, PR samples, buyer samples, and trade show product.

Be Organized

Keep an ongoing list of all your retailers with the following information:

- Number of Stores
- Name of Rep Company that calls on this account
- Date of first call
- Date of follow up communication to buyer and rep
- Test order quantities

- Promotional order quantities
- Planogram order quantities
- Ship Date
- In-store date
- Ad Date

How Long Does it Take to Manufacture Your Product?

Lead times (the time it takes to manufacture, ship and deliver the product) vary. Most products that are manufactured in China (that do not require a mold) have a ninety day lead time to reach your US warehouse.
- 30 days to order materials
- 30 days to manufacture the product
- 30 days to ship to your US port

If your product requires a mold to be made, allow for the mold time in your product development process. Mold Making is a time consuming process and can take three to nine months depending on the size and complication of the mold.

Once your mold is ready for production, the manufacturing process has a similar lead-time. Your factory, of course, will confirm actual ship dates.

Trade Shows

After you have researched the industry and have chosen a trade show to exhibit your products your next step is to reserve a booth space and participate in any promotional opportunities that are affordable and effective.

You will receive a show package along with your registrations materials. This package provides you with all the necessary information; power, set up times, cleaning services, labor, show events, exhibitors, PR room, etc.

Your Display Booth

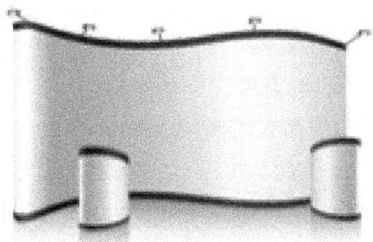

Your exhibit booth is a billboard for your brand and company image. The more professional your booth design, the more credible your brand and product is perceived.

You have three booth choices available to you:

- Use the trade show's standard booth space. This is usually a draped back wall and two draped side rails with a carpeted floor area. You can rent a six-foot table from the show exhibit company and provide your own product signage. They usually provide standard sign – your company name that hangs from the top back wall. This is the least expensive way to exhibit your product and it is also the least effective, as it does not feature your logo, company image and brand.

- Rent a booth from an exhibit booth company. You can rent a ten-foot pop up booth which is very affordable and provides you with a back wall unit on which you can affix your company logo. These wall units also accommodate shelf units if required. You can choose a booth color that is more in keeping with your brand image. These booths often come with a podium in the same color as the booth. The exhibit company can produce your company logo and provide any additional signage for a relatively inexpensive cost. These booths are quick and easy to set up and do not require additional labor. At our first Caboodles trade show, this is the booth design we used. WE chose a black pop up booth with a colorful Velcro Caboodles logo. We also purchased a black carpet for the floor area. We featured products on shelves attached to the back wall unit. The bright colored boxes worked well against the black background.

- Have a customized booth built. This is obviously the most effective way to display your brand and company image - but the most expensive. For another of our product lines we purchased a 10ft x 10f custom booth which cost us approx. $15,000. We also had decided to exhibit at a trade show "at the last minute" and had only one week to have our booth built. Utilizing available materials from our exhibit company, we had them create a customized booth complete with light box photos of our products and company logo. We chose a bright yellow for the booth and floor tiles. The back walls were slotted to accommodate both shelves and peg units. The result was fantastic. The brand came to life, the company looked professional, and the products in their bright purple packaging created the necessary contrast. Large corporations attending the trade shows have huge, custom designed exhibit areas costing hundreds of thousands of dollars. These booth areas have meeting rooms, multiple levels, upstairs coffee patios, and impressive brand advertising billboards.

Designing Your Booth

If you have decided to have a customized booth designed there are three major elements to consider:

Firstly; Color – choose a color that incorporates your band image and enables you to show your product to its best advantage.

Secondly: Product display area. Make your booth design flexible enough to accommodate different display options (i.e. shelves, pegs, etc.)

Thirdly: Brand and product images. A lighted center back panel allows you to feature your brand logo and a small selection of your products very effectively. Photos can be changed periodically to keep your booth design updated along with your new product introductions each year.

Setting Up Your Booth

There will be specified set up days prior to the show opening date. If your booth requires labor to erect your booth, you may be required to use the union labor provided at a cost through the trade show authorities.

Check your show guide for details. If you are using their draped booth display or you have a simple pop up booth you can set up your booth yourself. Allow plenty of time to set up your products and display materials.

Always create a list of all the products you will be exhibiting at the show and make a rough sketch of where they will be displayed within the booth. Take extra product and display materials with you. It is a fine balance between creating a "clean image" and displaying enough merchandise to establish credibility with your customers.

Whenever I make a presentation for a new line of products I am always establishing planogram credibility. What you visually present is what your customer is visually absorbing. If you present one product your customer sees one product sitting on the shelf. If you present a two foot section of product, your customer sees a two foot section in the store and so on.

If you have merchandising display units (POPs) available feature these displays in your booth. It shows your customers a way to bring your products into their stores without them having to find precious shelf space.

Make sure you have all your sales materials ready. I would create a simple one or two page catalog from my sales book information. You will need to color copy a hundred sets for give a ways at the show.

We often offer a show special price sheet with a discounted price for customers who place orders at the show or immediately after the show.

You do not want to give out catalogs or price sheets to anyone who is not a potential customer - particularly not your competition. Keep your sales materials out of sight and only distribute these to customers who are willing to give you their business cards or identify themselves as a retailer customer. You can always suggest emailing information to customers who do not want to be carrying around materials at the show.

Meeting Your Customers (buyers)

Your product presentations should be short and informative. A quick overall summary of what your product is, what is the suggested retail, what it does and who is your targeted consumer is what they want to hear.

No show attendee has time for a drawn out sales pitch. If your consumer gives your product four and a half seconds attention on the retail shelf, then know that your customer is giving your product a similar glance as he is walking the show.

The end result is to have obtained the potential customer's business card, provided a catalog and price sheet, and to have established their interest in purchasing your line. The rest is up to you and your rep in the follow up procedure after the show.

If, however, the customer wants to write an order there and then, be prepared.

Take notes during the show. At the end of each day, I usually type up a detailed report of who visited our booth, what the response has been important follow up information and so on. These notes are very valuable for the follow up process.

I have always looked forward to our trade shows with a sense of anticipation and expectation. This is the time for a product developer, brand developer and market to present their new products, new promotions and new ad campaigns to the marketplace. Buyers from around the world attend the major shows and, at many shows, our product lines have proven to be the most exciting products at the show. When Caboodles introduced Jellies at the NACDS trade show, buyers were excited to see innovation in the category and the sales reflected their enthusiasm.

One year, at the Housewares Show in Chicago, our company was introducing a number of new products including a talking horoscope clock. The next morning on Good Morning America, Dolly Parton was the guest on the show and our clock was sitting on the coffee table in front of her. She loved our product and it was so exciting to see one of our new inventions being shown on National TV. This product also featured on CNN the next day as "one of the hot products at the show".

Hiring and Meeting Your Reps

As mentioned before, trade shows are an opportune time to meet with potential sales reps who may be interested in representing your line. Take this opportunity to interview these reps and go through your product line with them. Interested reps may also bring potential buyers to your booth.

If you already have your rep force in place, your reps may have arranged scheduled meetings with buyers at designated times during the show.

By the time you are attending your fourth and fifth trade show, your appointment book will be busy with appointments.

Often we would hold our national sales meetings a day before the show or following the show taking advantage of all our reps being in the same town.

PR at the Show

Most trade shows have a designated press room. Obtain a list of attending media personnel from your trade show organization and have the required number of press releases delivered to the press room prior to the opening day of the show.

Appointments can be made by your PR agency with industry media personnel during the show.

Other Exhibitors

You may have other company exhibitors interested in doing joint promotions with your product. Or maybe simply interested in receiving product samples for their own use. Obviously companies that compete with you in any way should not have access to your product information. However, often manufacturers that are selling to your customers in the same industry are some of your best allies and the more your product is talked about in the industry the better it is for you.

Follow Up After the Show

Once you are back in your office after the show you will be busy with your follow up letters (emails) to interested customers.

Sort your collection of business cards into specific groups: retailers, distributors, reps, media (trade and consumer) and manufacturers.

Write your follow up emails immediately following the show. Don't lose momentum. For a smaller retailer, enclose a catalog and price sheet and order form. The easier you make it for a customer to purchase your product, the more likely you are to get an order. If it is a major retailer, the order process is more complicated and an order form is not suggested. You will need to arrange a follow up meeting to discuss your program, product and their continued interest.

Follow up with interested sales reps. Send out independent rep contracts for execution to the reps you wish to hire. Obtain their company information, territories covered, accounts covered, etc. Keep files of each rep group and mark their territories on your wall map.

Establishing Yourself in the Marketplace

Keeping Ahead of the Competition

I am sure you have heard that imitation is the best form of flattery. The trick is to keep ahead of the competition. So as you are launching new products into the marketplace your competition will be copying your existing product.

Becoming number one is a lot easier than staying number one. I mentioned earlier about keeping your mind focused on your vision. Keeping your vision and growing your vision is a constant requirement if you are to be successful in brand and product development. If you lose focus your vision simply dissipates into thin air and often your products go with it.

By the time your category is established (usually two to three years), you should be buying your product from the factories in large enough volume that your costs will be hard to beat.

How Do You Know What Inventory is Enough?

Most retailers know what "turns" (i.e. how many times a year they have to replenish the order due to sell through) are expected in your product category. Some items turn four to six times a year, others a little more, others a little less. Filling a planogram can generate a very large order. So, as mentioned earlier, before a buyer, or you, commit to a planogram your product is usually tested first. During the test your product is usually displayed in a promotional area such as in a free-standing display unit or in a seasonal isle (Easter, Halloween, Back to School). The buyer may choose a small selection of Stores (ten to twenty) to test your product.

If the test proves successful, then the buyer may decide to put your product in the planogram. Usually planograms are set early in the year (January through March).

A great time to test your product is Holiday. This is the biggest selling time of the year and if your product is in the store at this time you and the buyer will have a good indication of whether or not your product will make the following year's planogram.

Everyday Item Means Everyday Sales

Is your product a seasonal item or an everyday item? If it is a seasonal item make sure you have an item for every season. Preferably you want to create an "everyday item". No retailer is going to planogram your product line if it only has a short life span of one season. A planogram (which is where you make the most money) is set in the store for at least a six months period. Usually you can update your items within the same shelf space for another six months giving you a full year of real estate to generate sales for the retailer and yourself. Just because you are an "everyday item" does not mean you cannot participate in seasonal/promotional opportunities in the store. Your buyer may choose one or two of your new items to promote on an end cap giving you both promotional and everyday space. You may also be able to create a special promotion utilizing your product (free cosmetics with a Caboodles organizer) to stimulate additional promotional space.

Earning Your Real Estate

This real estate has to be earned by good sell through. If you are going to make the planogram next year with a new selection of your branded products, then your products have to be proven winners.

Now you are beginning to understand the importance of product lines versus a single product and a brand versus non branded products. You are also understanding why you have to keep updating your products and adding new products to your product line.

Keeping Your Product Updated

It often depends on the product category as to what percentage of your line needs to be changed each year. In cosmetics, for example, 80% of the line remains fairly much the same – new colors and ingredients are updated but the basic items remain the same. That leaves 20% for product innovation – new items, new packaging, etc.

In some categories all product colors change once or twice a year and, in order to increase your shelf space (or replace slow selling items) new items are added throughout the year. Some new items may be tested first before making it to the planogram.

Usually the 80/20 rule applies. Imagine if you visited your local discounter store and all the product looked the same as last year. Fashion changes, trends change, colors change, and product change.

The Changing Face of Retail

It is a new era in retail as the line between virtual and physical space becomes challenged. Consumers want online coupons, and to take advantage of Flash Sales (time-limited offers of high discounts). Within the last couple of decades consumers are increasingly taking advantage of this faster, cheaper and more convenient way of shopping.

When I first called on retailers, our meetings consisted of 90% new product discussions and 10% business. Buyers were as excited about new product innovation as we were.

Today, it is a different story. Buyers are pressed to make their numbers as their computers have become their masters. Every product is judged on gross profit and turns. Today's meetings are 90% business and 10% innovation. Although new product has lots its place as a major focus, without it, merchandise on the shelf would become stagnant and old. New products are the life blood of retail.

I am seeing, however, the wheel slowly turning and new products, new categories and new brands returning back into focus. Just a few years ago, a large drug chain re-opened their new vendor buying days after a five-year closed-door policy. They were looking, once again, for something exciting and new. Vendors lined up at the font doors waiting for the doors to open for the opportunity to show their new products.

Today you have new opportunities to promote your product to your customers. Buyers can simply log on and check out your website and our full range of products. Your website becomes your virtual brand identity. You still need your printed catalogs, sell sheets and price sheets for your reps and buyers, but your website gives you the opportunity to keep your company, brand and products fresh, exciting and current. Your website quickly directs your online shoppers to the retailers who carry your products.

Daily informative product/trend tweets directing consumers to "shop now" and "product in use videos" keep your brand and products relevant into today's social media world. Make sure you have a number of customer review videos for your YouTube consumers – a wonderful PR tool that gives your brand and product instant credibility.

Retail buyers are some of the hardest working people I know. Many buyers rely on our reps to assist with paperwork, projections, product allocations etc.

Your traditional retail customers are becoming few and few. Twenty-five years ago I used to call on one hundred and forty buyers a year throughout the United States. I was on the road three hundred days a year. When I wasn't on the road, I was creating and marketing the products and the brand. Today, many smaller retailers have been bought by larger retailers.

Some retailers have simply gone out of business. Some retailers have become stronger and more powerful. Most retailers have both a virtual and physical presence giving your product more exposure than ever before.

The Opportunity is Still There

There are still many thousands of major discount and drug stores in the USA today. It may take you three years, even with a winning brand and a continued flow of innovation, to obtain distribution in the majority of these accounts. But you only need a few of the major retailers to planogram your items to be in a multi million dollar business.

Retail Chains in the USA

The International Mass Retail Association (IMRA) represents one hundred and seventy mass retailers that include discount department stores, home centers, catalog showrooms, dollar stores, variety stores, warehouse clubs, deep discount drug stores, specialty discounters and off-price stores. Collectively, IMRA retail members operate more than 54,000 stores in the USA and abroad and employ over a million people.

Drug Store Chains have a large number of stores but do less volume and have slower turns in general merchandise. So although the sell-in is substantial the re-orders are much smaller than the mass retailers.

Do research online, - you can gather up to date store count information at a glance.

Selling Your Product Worldwide

Selling your line internationally makes sense if your product is manufactured in China. It is cost effective for your customers to purchase the product straight from China. International customers are always looking for what is hot and what is new. At times I feel that the international market is where America used to be twenty-five years ago, with a focus on innovation and opportunity.

If the product is manufactured in the USA it is often necessary to set up manufacturing facilities in the individual countries in order to eliminate the incurred freight costs. This is time consuming and little over whelming to say the least.

I recommend international distribution for two reasons. One: because I am a New Zealander and understand the importance of increasing your sales volume internationally as well as nationally. (In New Zealand the only product I could sell to the mass market would have to be purchased by our thirty million sheep and thirty million cattle as our human population is only four million.) And two: an international brand vs. a national brand has a greater value. Increased distribution means increased sales.

When, and if, you decide to sell your brand or your company after a minimum of three years, your international distribution not only increases your value but could also entice an international buyer.

Why Would Other Countries Purchase Your Product and Not simply Knock it Off?

International distributors or retailers are looking for product lines that are exciting, affordable and new. If they can purchase the product line from you for a fair price then they would much rather do this than take the risk of creating their own product line. Plus, it takes time and money to develop and market a brand. They understand branding and understand they are not just buying a line of products from you (which they could copy if they so desired) but are buying a branded line of products that you will continually keep updated and new. They will also be looking for the new items in six months along with your domestic retailers.

Licensing Your Brand Name

Branding your product line not only enables you to take your product idea into multiple categories, but also opens up the opportunity of licensing your brand name to other manufacturers who will, in turn, use your brand name to market and sell their own products.

Of course this takes time, usually a number of years, before your brand has developed enough consumer awareness to be of value to other companies.

Licensing your brand not only generates additional revenue to your company through licensing fees, but allows you, the licensor, to enter additional categories that your company may not have the expertise or the necessary capital to enter alone.

When your brand awareness has matured and you are ready to enter the licensing arena there are excellent licensing agents who will pursue compatible viable companies on your behalf for a percentage of the licensing fees. A three-year renewable contract, based on required sales levels allows you the flexibility to cancel the contract if certain sales are not generated within a particular time frame, leaving you the opportunity to source another licensee for this product category if you so desire. The royalties generated from licensing your brand name can be very lucrative.

Licensing fees differ depending on the particular category and the strength of your brand.

Licensing fees can range from 4% to 15% with most product categories falling within the 5% - 7% range.

This means if you license your brand name to a company doing twenty million dollars annually in your branded product sales, under a 5% licensing agreement, your company generates one million dollars annually in royalty revenue. (less your agent's percentage of 20% - 30% of your take.)

Licensing Another Brand Name For Your Products

I am a believer that you need to develop your own brand before adding other brand names to your product category. If your product line is introduced using another brand name or brand names, you will have difficulty creating a value to your own brand - which tends to get lost in the shuffle.

However, there are exceptions to this rule. If your product idea needs instant brand or product recognition in order for it to be accepted by the retailer and the consumer, then adding an existing brand name to your products may be beneficial. If you have a children's toy that would have more impact on the shelf by carrying a recognizable brand name or character name then licensing may be the recommended way to go. For example, if you had an idea that involves innovative voice activated animal characters, you may choose to license Disney or Looney Tunes characters to give your products instant product recognition on the shelf. Disney or Looney Tunes would be the licensor and you would be the licensee and the royalty fees for any one of these major brand would be expensive.

You can still create your own brand name, such as voice activated, Chatting Critters, which enables you to take your idea into other categories. For example, the stationery category with your Chatting Critters in miniature size attached to the end of pens and pencils.

The big branded companies have their own product development divisions who are responsible for creating their own innovative new products and your item would need to be extremely desirable for them to even consider you as a licensee.

The cost factor can be cost prohibitive as licensing characters or other brand names adds cost to your products and therefore increases the retail price points and could stop you from being price competitive in the marketplace.

There is also an upfront licensing fee. Talk to a licensing agent about the costs involved and the feasibility of obtaining a license of you feel that this is the an option you want to pursue.

Don't forget to have everyone sign a confidentiality agreement and, if your idea is patentable, ensure you have all the legal documents included in your presentation materials.

How Much Does it Cost

Now we are ready to talk about financing your project. It is really simple to explain who gets what in a new business venture. Money equals ownership. It is that simple.

The longer you can wait to involve a capital investor the better it is for you.

As you develop your product concept into a viable, marketable product line you are creating a value. The further you get without having to raise outside capital, the more ownership you will have in the venture and the more likely you are to raise the required capital.

Hire a good attorney to negotiate with you and any potential investor opportunities. No matter what the deal is, make sure you have it in writing. You want to be covered legally even if it is a good friend loaning you money. Problems only usually arise when a product fails or is a great success. Look at the upside and the downside. Don't be greedy. A small percentage of a financially successful venture is better than a large percentage of a financial disaster. At the same time, you don't want to be giving away your business for less than what it is worth.

But be aware, many product ideas fail due to lack of working capital. A great idea without the financial ability to take it to market is a product going nowhere.

Only Raise Money When you Need It

Raise necessary capital as you require it because no matter how much you think you need, you will need more.

If ever you have built your own home you will know what I am talking about. Rule of thumb is: guesstimate the amount of capital you think you will and double it.

Taking a product to the mass market can cost anywhere from $50,000 to $100,000 if you are doing most of the product development process yourself and your product does not require expensive tooling. It can cost millions of dollars once you are in the manufacturing mode. But you will not be manufacturing large quantities without a major retailer's commitment and by then, you will be in a very strong position to raise the necessary capital without losing too much ownership in your company.

The best way to work out your initial costs is to keep a tally of what you need to purchase for the initial product and brand development stage. These costs depend on what you already own and what you will need to acquire.

Your product(s) idea, once created, copyrighted, and incorporated into a good business plan will assist you in raising the necessary capital.

Financing your Vision

There are usually four critical stages that require capital infusion.

First Stage: Early development – High Risk

These costs are minimal. Most of the work you will be doing yourself. Most of the costs relate to the tools you need to put your idea on paper.

A complete computer/scanner printer/camera/software package can cost just a few thousand dollars. (I have always used Mac computers as do most designers). This equipment will get you through the process from an idea to an image that you can work with.

You have yet to prove to yourself, let alone others, that you have a viable product. This stage is very high risk. Self-finance is recommended. Raising capital at this state is not only very difficult but can result in you giving up most of your ownership in the product, if not, all of your ownership.

So wait it out. Do most of the work yourself. You don't have anything to "sell" yet.

Before you get to the next stage you should have created a visual of your product idea/ expanded your idea into multiple products/ researched your industry and product category, obtained copies of legal documents for your protection and run focus groups to establish credibility for your invention.

If you need help getting your product onto paper, hire a graphic artist online through a company such as fiverr.com. When exposing your idea to others have them sign a confidentiality agreement.

Second Stage: Product Prototyping, Sampling, Trade Shows, Making Sales Presentations

Now you are at a stage when you will be requiring some working capital. Depending on your product, these costs can be kept to a minimum.

Raising capital is the same process as selling your product idea to a retailer. The more research you can provide to prove your product's viability, the more likely you are to obtain the finance you need.

By the time you have reached this stage in your product development you should have completed your industry research, created your brand identity, developed your product idea into a visual, have researched your manufacturing and warehouse options, and have completed your initial costing analysis.

Your product/brand/company book should

contain the following information:

- Product concept in illustration or sample form
- Industry, category and focus group research
- Brand, product line and product graphics (logos)
- List of potential retailers and distribution
- Sales projections – both short term (promotional opportunities) and long term (possible planograms)
- Marketing and PR information (i.e. consumer advertising, consumer shows, trade shows, website, press events)
- Projected expenses (i.e. mold costs, sample products, marketing, manufacturing, warehousing, shipping and handling, EDI, travel and sales materials.

Sales projections are just that, projections. They are not commitments from buyers. However, it is important for you to know what your potential sales could be. You need to know this for two reasons; firstly, to estimate the quantity of product you will need to manufacture/supply, and secondly, to know how much capital you will need to finance the manufacturing and distribution of your product.

To work out your potential sales you combine the results from your focus groups with the number of stores who could potentially carry your items.

If 85% of your focus group participants said they would purchase your product (an innovative baby carrier) and your consumer bas is four million (the number of pregnant women in the USA each year) then you have a consumer base of approximately 3.4 million.

Now, take a conservative number of stores that would carry baby carriers in the USA. If you add Wal-Mart, Target, Babies R Us, Toys R Us, and K-Mart the total is approximately eight thousand stores. This is not adding in Amazon.com and other online baby retailers, which is considerably more volume. You will know how many stores will carry your item from your previous research.

Now you have to tally in how many products (baby carriers) you will be selling into each store:

Let's say you have created two different colors (black and gingham) and have two different designs for a total of four products per store. That is 32,000 units if all these stores planogram your items. Of course you will have to keep the shelves stocked for a year and if we say your product turns three times a year that is 96,000 units.

If your baby carrier sells to the retailer for five dollars that is $495,000 in sales. If your manufacturing costs are $1.85 per unit then it will cost you $177,600 just to make the product. You still have the added costs related to setting up your business, warehousing, shipping, and, of course, all the store discounts we talked about earlier.

If your product is a phenomenal success (like Caboodles) and you get distribution into 30,000 stores with twelve to twenty-four products per store and your product turns four times per year you can see how you can easily end up in the multi million unit category.

Initially though, you are more likely to just get

"tests" in the stores. This is a lot more manageable as you will be shipping in limited quantities to a limited number of stores to see if your product sells enough volume to warrant a planogram. But, be prepared, If your item is a winner going out the gate, then you will need some serious capital behind you.

Why your consumer base is important is because it indicates how big your potential business could be. If your consumer base is 3.4 million and 50% of these consumers purchase your product every year (babies are born every year), you could sell 1.7 million products at five dollars for a total of $8.5 million per year.

You can understand now why you had to do all that initial research into your product category, number of retailers, number of stores, who your consumer is and how many potential consumer would purchase your product.

Knowing your consumer base is also important when it comes to overestimating your potential sales. You are dreaming if you think you can sell in five million units to retailers if your consumer base is only four million.

Therefore, it is important that you have a product that you keep updated and innovative every year. This encourages your consumer to keep purchasing your products year in and year out. With Caboodles our targeted teen consumer was purchasing more than one product per year due to fashion colors and trends. It was imperative that we kept the category alive with new styles, new colors and new sizes.

At this stage, however, you are only looking for enough capital to take your product on the road, Once you begin to receive verbal commitments to purchaser your product you will need to raise additional finance but your value in the venture has increased tenfold and finance will be easier to raise and cost you less.

Travel will be one of your major expenses during this portion of your journey. Traveling to meet with reps and even buyers (if you have developed your product idea in a presentable prototype or sample) will need to be budgeted for. When I was traveling across the country three hundred days a year for the first few years, my traveling expenses topped well over $100,000 per year.

Your other costs will be for your prototypes, packaging mockups, and samples. These costs relate directly to what type of product you are creating. You will have researched these costs by now and have a good indication of what these expenses are.

By now you have already decided on what trade and consumer shows you wish to attend and have budgeted for their exhibit fees and your booth costs.

Third Stage: Manufacturing, Warehousing, and Shipping

When you have reached this stage in your journey it is

a lot easier to raise finance as you have already received verbal commitments to purchase from retailers or, at the very least, have received such favorable response in the marketplace that you are prepared to begin the manufacturing process.

You also have a choice at a crossroads. You can choose three different directions:

• You can sell your idea to a manufacturer who may be prepared to invest in your product for a piece of the action (shares in your company). He may be prepared to invest some capital and/or assist with the manufacturing costs. This will require a partnership agreement or appropriate written contract stating the terms of the agreement.

• License your product to a manufacturer who would pay you a royalty and take over the manufacturing, warehousing, shipping, sales and marketing, customer service, etc. You simply hand over the product to them (with a solid licensing agreement in place (and you will no longer need to raise any more capital.

• You can raise outside capital and simply continue paying for all the expenses associated with manufacturing, warehousing, shipping and selling and marketing your product and brand. You will have already sourced Custom Manufacturers and have received per unit manufacturing quotes.

You will definitely need a substantial capital investment in order to proceed at this juncture if you are going it alone.

Not only will you need money to actually manufacture your product and for the associated costs in getting products to your retailers, but you will need a line of credit at the bank to cover any large orders you may receive. If you are not in the position to provide the security yourself then you will need an investor to do this for you. An investor will take a percentage in your product (or company) in return for providing the necessary cash flow.

It takes ninety days from placing an order with your factory in China to it arriving in your US warehouse and you will not be receiving an actual written order until thirty days before the product needs to arrive in their stores. Most retailers pay thirty to sixty days. At holiday some retailers request ninety days dating. This means that you will require some bridging finance as you will need to pay your factory ninety to hundred and twenty days before you will be getting paid.

Once you actually receive a written order you can arrange **factoring** (a finance institution will loan you the money for a monthly interest fee) providing the retailer is in a good financial situation. This brings the period when you will need bridging finance to approximately sixty days.

This is a good time to work with a financial adviser to look at all your options.

Stage Four: Building a Company and Building Inventory for Planograms

You are on you way now and hopefully you have not had to give away all your ownership in your product line, brand, or company in order to get here.

Every time you raise capital, you lose ownership. But doing it in stages is often less painful financially than raising it all at the beginning.

Now you have a company that is worth something. Your product has proven itself in the marketplace. Your company is generating sales. You have an asset. You have real estate at retail. You have a product line. You have a brand. You should also be working on your next season's product line. You have something to sell now.

Raising capital at this stage is less difficult and less costly. And you have more choices open to you.

Building up staff is now essential to operate our business effectively - a national sales manager, customer service personnel, financial staff, inventory manager, etc.

The next big cash infusion may be needed for company growth. This is usually in its third year.

You may choose to do an IPO or sell the company as a going concern. If your dream is to sell your company and/or brand and product lines and cash out you can't expect this to happen until at least your business is in its third year. Most major companies do not even consider purchasing a brand until it has proven itself in the marketplace and all the kinks have been ironed out.

Cashing out is definitely an option of your company is profitable and generating good sales. Even if it is not particularly profitable but has national and international distribution and your next few years projections are feasibly you may still have a valuable asset to sell.

Many entrepreneurs tend to get bored when a product idea matures into a sizable business. Often entrepreneurs make the worst general managers as their heart is in the initial creating and building of the brand and this usually where their talent lies. Running a company is a skill in itself. Smart entrepreneurs hire General Mangers to run their companies.

Often the money that has been raised during the life of the company has come complete with financial and managing directors who are involved heavily in the day to day operations of the business in order to protect their investment.

When you are in need of investment capital throughout the life of your company it is wise to know "who you will be in bed with" for the next few years. Make sure that your talents are complimentary not conflicting as choosing the right partner is often as important as raising the capital.

If your company has reached the three-year growth stage you also have the option to do an IPO (independent Public Offering). This is an excellent way to generate cash flow. You can hire a financial institution that will assist you with this process.

You also have the choice to simply find an investor at this stage to assist you thought the next big growth period of continuing to build your brand and product lines. However, it is usually recommended to "sell out" just before your business reaches it s peak. Often a larger, more structured corporation has the necessary skills and personnel required to take a brand from a fifteen to thirty million dollar brand (a small company) to a one hundred plus million dollar brand.

Large corporations grow by acquisitions and once your company proves itself and is profitable – being acquired by a large corporation is another very attractive option. And a wonderful way out of an old idea so you can concentrate on your new one.

The Third Year Curse

Every successful product, brand, or company is carried forward by the energy of its creator. Keep hands on and focused throughout your product's journey. I have seen product lines just dissipate when the owner or creator's focus has waned. That said, there is a time (usually in three to five years) when a company has matured from a start-up entrepreneurial focus to a low-risk, high functioning, more-corporate focus. When this happens, the inventor, developer, marketer and wiz kid who grew the company from zero to millions is no longer the hero but often becomes the loose canon - resulting in a "parting of the ways".

I have seen this happen so often and in so many different type companies. A word of advice, after three years take a close look at your position and decide if it is time for you to "cash out". Often this is the time when the growth of the company has resulted in a management team and board of directors comprised of "investment capital providers". Entrepreneurs are starters, innovators, developers and risk takers. Most companies would never have existed without them. However, entrepreneurs don't always make great corporate CEOs. Most entrepreneurs don't want to be CEOs.

Get out that book "Who Ate My Cheese" and check you are not stamping your foot and saying, "It is my cheese! I found it! It is mine! And I am not leaving! I deserve it! Sometimes it is time to find fresh cheese before there is no cheese to be had.

Conclusion

Treasure your successes and honor your creative gifts. To an entrepreneur the end of one venture is the beginning of another.

In order to be a successful product developer and marketer you have to be able to take an idea from conception to completion. Having the ability to complete a project as to be one of your personality traits.

Every stage of your journey takes enthusiasm and tenacity. Completing all other steps required to successfully launch your product into the marketplace takes courage and belief in your own vision. Information can be researched, finance can be obtained, products can be made, manufacturing can be sourced, orders can be written, products can be shipped and companies can be staffed.

Visions or ideas are gifts. They cannot be found in a book or learned in a classroom. They are elusive and fragile in their infancy and their survival is dependent on your constant focus and attention.

As I mentioned at the beginning of this book, you can take a camel to water but you can't make him drink. Only the end consumer can make your product a success.

I wish you well on your own journey. Have fun along the way. Don't let your pride get in the way, get professional help when you need it, ask questions and remember to stop and enjoy your successes as they happen. And, please protect yourself legally throughout all aspects of your creative and business ventures.

If you found this book helpful, I would love you to leave a review on Amazon.   Thank you.

About the Author

Puppeteer, children's entertainer, owner of a model agency, TV talk show panelist, luxury accommodation owner, entrepreneur, product developer, brand developer, storyteller, author and indie publisher, Leonie Mateer has lived a full and diverse life.

Born and raised in New Zealand, Mateer moved to the United States in her 30s to pursue business opportunities.

She returned to New Zealand for several years in the 2000s, running a luxury lodge in Northland – which has been an inspiration for her crime series – and now splits her time between Northland, New Zealand and the United States.

Mateer is known for her huge success as a brand development expert. She was named in the 'Who's Who' of both Leading American Executives and American Inventors in the 1990s.

Creator of the brand, Caboodles™ - a teen girl brand that took the retail industry by storm in the late 1980s and early 90s. Caboodles created a new category at retail "The Cosmetics Organizer Category" with global retail sales exceeding $100 million worldwide

THE CABOODLES BLUEPRINT – TURN YOUR IDEA INTO MILLIONS has just been re-released.

"HAVE A PRODUCT IDEA? - HOW MANY COULD YOU SELL? - a collection of business articles she has written and which have generated hundreds of thousands of readers over the past many years. Each chapter is a product development and marketing gem - from tips for protecting your idea to getting your product on the shelves of Wal-Mart, Target, K-Mart and more...

PSORIASIS – THE SIMPLE CURE – WHO KNEW? Is her first health and wellness book.

Over 120 million people worldwide suffer from psoriasis.

Leonie Mateer tells her story with honesty and stark humility. Living with a socially and personally disfiguring disease she offers her readers twenty-five years of research into how to eliminate the effects of **plaque psoriasis** and PSA. She tells of tried and tested cures from crystals, coal tar and ointments to almost every drug available. She finally finds the cure in the most unexpected place.

A must read for any psoriasis sufferer.

She has also written and published THE AUDREY MURDERS – a five book thriller series, starring Audrey, a serial killer living in idyllic small-town New Zealand.

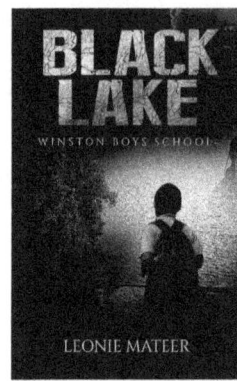 

Other books include:
THE MAGICAL WORLD OF DANTONIA (mid-grade),
BLACK LAKE (mid-grade),

Both books written for her grandchildren.

READ YOUR OWN FORTUNE
READ YOUR OWN FINANCIAL FORTUNE
(spiritual, new age, self help)

Leonie's two daughters and four grandsons live in the United States and are a constant inspiration for many of her stories.

THE CABOODLES BLUEPRINT

www.ingramcontent.com/pod-product-compliance
Lightning Source LLC
Chambersburg PA
CBHW031543040426
42452CB00006B/168